THE
DRUNKEN
UNIVERSE

An Anthology of
Persian Sufi Poetry

*Translations and Commentary
by Peter Lamborn Wilson
and Nasrollah Pourjavady*

OMEGA PUBLICATIONS
NEW LEBANON

AUTHORS' ACKNOWLEDGMENT

The translation and commentary were prepared with the assistance
of the program "Philosophy and World Community," edited by
Raymond Klibansky, under the auspices of
the International Institute of Philosophy,
the International Federation of Philosophical Societies, and
the Conseil International de le Philosophie
et des Sciences Humanines,
with the support of UNESCO.

First published 1987 by Phanes Press,
Grand Rapids, Michigan

New edition published December 1999 by
Omega Publications
256 Darrow Road
New Lebanon New York 12125-2615

Cover design by Abi'l-Khayr and Tom Stier.
Book design by Abi'l-Khayr.

Printed in the United States of America
ISBN 0-930872-65-65-7

We invite you to explore other materials
drawn from the Sufi tradition
at our website:
www.wisdomschild.com

*Musician, play me a melody
to make me greatly sigh,*

*Utter a verse to make me pour upon the dust
this flagon of wine.*

–Hafiz

CONTENTS

INTRODUCTION

Poetry

Of all the strands of thought, tradition, and belief that make up the Islamic universe, Sufism in its doctrinal aspect stands out as the most intact, the most purely Islamic: the central strand. Opponents of Sufism often charge it with having originated outside Islam, but a close study of the various schools of philosophy and theology, and a comparison with "primordial" Islam as revealed in the Koran and hadith (authentic sayings of the Prophet Mohammad), will vindicate the Sufis' claim of centrality, of strict adherence to the original purity of the Revelation.

In the context of the history of thought, in fact, Sufism—always insisting on a return to the sources of the Tradition—can be seen to have functioned at times as a positive and healthy reaction to the overly rational activity of the philosophers and theologians. For the Sufis, the road to spiritual knowledge—to Certainty—could never be confined to the process of rational or purely intellectual activity, without sapiential knowledge (*zawq*, "taste") and the direct, immediate experience of the Heart. Truth, they believed, can be sought and found only with one's entire being; nor were they satisfied merely to *know* this Truth. They insisted on a total identification with it: a "passing away" of the knower in the Known, of subject in the Object of knowledge. Thus,

1

fourth/tenth-century* Sufi Hallaj proclaimed "I am the Truth" (and was martyred for it by the exoteric authorities), he was not violating the "First Pillar" of Islam, the belief in Unity *(tawhid)*, but simply stating the truth from the mouth of the Truth. So the Sufis believe.

This insistence on total involvement in "mystical" realization, and on a participative understanding of religious doctrine, sharply distinguished Sufism from other Islamic schools of thought. In fact, considering themselves the true core of Islam, Sufis appeared as outsiders not only to the philosophers and theologians, but even to "ordinary" Muslims. Their peculiarity, their distinctness, manifested itself in every aspect of their lives: their daily activities, their worship, social relations, and even style or means of expression. Like mystics in all Traditions, they tended to remake language and form for their own purposes, and as in all Traditional civilizations, the potency and directness of their expression tended to flow out and permeate other areas not directly related to mysticism in the narrow sense: literature, the arts and crafts, etc. In this book we are concerned with one art that the Sufis made peculiarly their own: poetry.

In the first century or two after the Prophet, the Sufis, if they wrote at all, tended to produce treatises and books in the same style as that of other theologians, differing only in their emphasis or content. More often, they avoided writing altogether, transmitting their teachings orally, through tales and fables or stories about saints and prophets. This method was quite in keeping

2

with the overwhelmingly Koranic style of early Islam, and in terms of this style the use of poetry appeared as something of a novelty.

This development occurred first in the Iraqi or "Baghdad" school of Sufism around the third/ninth century, and is exemplified by the writings of Hallaj and the woman saint Rabe'ah of Basra. The Sufis began to employ the old-fashioned vocabulary of the Arabic love songs in a new way in order to express their emotions, spiritual realizations, and "theology of Divine Love." In Iran, poetry began to develop in court circles, but the Sufis of Khorasan imitated the Iraqis in making use of a "profane" vocabulary, first in composing songs accompanied by musical instruments for their gatherings, gradually turning the forms toward the symbolic expression of purely metaphysical and mystical ideas.

The earliest verse forms thus used appear to have been various types of quatrains. Improvised by shaykhs in ecstasy or to make a point in their sermons, the great body of this literature from the fifth/eleventh century is of unknown authorship, though much of it is attributed to the great Abu Sa'id Abo'l-Khayr (357/967-440/1049), said by some people to have been the first Persian Sufi poet. Hakim Sana'i (died around 528/1133) was the first really major literary figure of Persian Sufism; he employed the full range of verse forms and meters and opened great new possibilities of expression.[1] After him, a veritable army of poets appears. 'Attar, Rumi, Sa'di, and Hafez have been introduced to Western readers, but they are only the vanguard, crests on the waves of a great sea of art.

Why should Sufis in general, and Persian Sufis in particular, choose to write poetry? One might simply answer that it satisfied their needs, as it did those of Parmenides. Or one might emphasize Islam as the Religion of the Word ("of the Book") and make a claim for poetry—after the Revelation itself—as the quintessence of language. Philosophers, theologians, and other groups of Muslim intellectuals such as the scientists and religious canonists *(foqahā)* employed prose, and so too did the Sufis—as one school among many. But when they wanted to "be themselves," lovers of the Truth, they needed a different language, more intense, closer to the center of human awareness than prose. Truth is beautiful, so when one speaks of it, one speaks beautifully. As the lover sings—almost by nature it would seem—to his beloved, so did the Sufis to theirs. Love itself creates a taste for this language, so that even the prose writers of Sufism, such as Ahmad Ghazāli or his disciple 'Ayn al-Qozāt Hamadāni, scatter verse throughout their works and create poetic prose.

This poetic consciousness sets Sufism apart, and indeed it was often used quite deliberately to emphasize the gulf between the Sufi way of thinking and that of the philosophers and theologians, dry and overly rational, prosaic. To the logic of the schools the Sufis opposed a logic of the Heart. To the confining sanity of ordinary thought they opposed a liberating music, a force capable

4

of breaking through the congealed ice of the mundane world, a power they sometimes identified with madness—since it appeared as such to their enemies.

Aside from didactic poems dealing with practical aspects of the Path or with what might be called Sufi ethics, the overwhelming theme of this poetry is the Love relationship between the individual [the lover] and his Beloved [God]. What characterizes the lover is his yearning or desire, his need. What characterizes the Beloved is beauty, loveliness, His self-sufficiency or needlessness. In love, the lover experiences the beauty of the Beloved, an experience that demands for its fullest realization the extinction of the lover's base qualities, and finally of his separative self or "ego." The intoxicating aspect of this experience suggests another set of metaphors to the poet, those revolving around wine and drunkenness. The very fact that wine is forbidden in Islam (but promised in paradise) adds to the power of this symbolism. But there are other reasons for using the symbols of love and wine.

The *Golshan-i raz* of Mahmud Shabestari (born 687/1288) is devoted to a hermeneutic of this symbolism of intoxication and the "physiognomy of Love";[2] here and elsewhere, the Sufis explain that there are two ways of looking at symbolism.

The first might be called Symbol-as-bridge (from the saying "The metaphor is a bridge to Reality"). Since the "real" experience of the mystic cannot be expressed in "mere words," the Sufis use an already existing terminology that bears some resemblance to or evokes some echo of their actual state. In this way of looking at the affair, words are first coined to apply to "worldly" things and then used by extension to refer to Divine Truths.

But the Koran tells us that God "taught Adam the Names," which implies that these Names are themselves aspects of the Divine that precede the phenomenal world or Creation. Like Plato's Ideas, these words are original and authentic; they are coined, as it were, by God to refer to Himself and are applied to things in the realm of multiplicity only by extension. Mohammad Ghazāli, in his *Niche for Lights*[3] turns this mode of understanding to an explanation of the word *Light (nur)*, which he says can be used properly only of God, and only metaphorically of actual physical light. *Existence, Love,* and other such key terms ultimately describe the Divine, and in the world can only be considered reflections or borrowings.

Of course these two ways of looking at symbolism are not mutually exclusive. In mathematics the mind solves a problem by working toward a solution; but in order to express the proof it then reverses the process. Similarly, one first experiences love or beauty as it exists "in the world" and works from this experience toward Divine Reality. Man begins his discovery of these things at the very end point of Divine Emanation, for man is "in exile" and must "return to the Origin." One might say, therefore, that the first way of understanding symbolism

6

is valid from man's point of view, the second from God's point of view——although ultimately Reality is One, and the very idea of there being more than one point of view is merely a separative illusion.

Sufism uses language in order to shatter this illusion, but to do so it must begin where man finds himself. To bridge the gap separating man's point of view and God's point of view, it must find a world between them, a world where God's Light is "parceled out" to lend existence to the myriad things, and where by reversing the process the myriad things can be "reunited" with that Light. This in-between-world or isthmus *(barzakh)* is the world of the archetypes, the "Imaginal World" that validates the symbolism of Sufi poetry. One might say that the language of the Sufis ("the language of the birds") impels us upward in flight toward this world, where the force of Divine attraction takes over and draws us up to the Real World, the realm of Unity. This double action, however, like all dualities, is again an illusion. It is God who "works" from the very beginning, for it is He, after all, Who inspires the true poet in the first place.

There exist any number of ways to approach a philosophical understanding of the language of Persian Sufi poetry, but certainly one of the most fruitful would be to read it in the light of systems propounded by thinkers who themselves developed and refined that language. In our commentaries on the poems, we have relied on two great figures in Sufism: Ahmad Ghazāli and Ibn 'Arabi.

Ahmad Ghazāli was the brother of Imam Mohammad Ghazāli, the great philosopher (or antiphilosopher) who devoted his brilliant career to a reconciliation between Sufism and orthodox theology. Algazel, as the Europeans called him, was not, however, an initiating shaykh, whereas Ahmad's name appears in the *silsilah*, or chain of transmission, of most of the Sufi orders in existence today. Furthermore, Ahmad's little treatise, the *Sawāneh*[4] had an influence on Sufi poetry as great as the general influence on Islamic thought of his brother's magnum opus, *The Revival of Religious Sciences*. The *Sawāneh is* a mixture of poetry and poetic prose. It deals with the symbolism of Love, but in a much more profoundly metaphysical way than anyone had done before (it appeared in about 508/1113). In effect, Ahmad treated the word *Love* almost as his brother treated the word *Light* in *The Niche for Lights*: as an all-sufficing, metaphysical ground for expressing a complete mystical philosophy. Just as later writers such as Sohrawardi extended Light symbolism into just such a universal philosophy,[5] so many later writers were to take up and extend Ahmad's Love symbolism, and even many of his specific images and tropes.

Ibn 'Arabi was not Persian—in fact he was a Spanish Arab—but his philosophy (or rather theosophy) penetrated Persia through his great disciple Sadroddin Qonawi[6] and through Persian poets such as Awhadoddin Kermāni and Fakhroddin 'Erāqi,[7] who devoted themselves to a synthesis of Ibn 'Arabi's teachings with the School of Love typified by Ahmad Ghazāli. The key word in Ibn 'Arabi is *Existence*, and his doctrine is known as *wahdat al-wojud*, the Unity of Existence. The first principle of faith, Unity *(tawhid)*, is used to resolve the theological problem of God's simultaneous immanence and transcendence by an insistence on absolute and radical oneness of Being. "There is no god but God" becomes for Ibn 'Arabi the starting point and ending point of a philosophical project so vast that it called for the composition of a staggering eight hundred books, some of them comprising many volumes. Although a great deal remains to be done to uncover this project in all its immensity, enough has appeared in English to excuse us from attempting a resumé in this Introduction.[8] It remains to be said, however, that although Ibn 'Arabi's system is based on a philosophy of Existence, he himself wrote one of the most beautiful and important books of Sufi love poetry,[9] in which he declared:

> *My heart embraces every form:*
> *pasture for gazelles*
> *convent for monks*
> *temple for idols*
> *Kaaba for pilgrims*
> *tables of the Torah*
> *pages of the Koran.*
> *I follow the Way of Love*
> *and where Love's caravan takes its path*
> *there is my religion, my faith.*

Thus Ibn 'Arabi is not only the exponent of the Unity of Being, and the transcendent unity of religions,[10] he is also a master of the Way of Love. His multifaceted teaching embraced the intuitive and Heart-centered world of poetry, and it was thus inevitable that he would be taken in and embraced by the Persians of the School of Love.

The Poems

You must take these poems as mirrors; for you know that a mirror has no form of itself, but rather reflects the face of anyone who looks in it. Just so, a poem has no one particular meaning of itself, but presents to each reader his state of the moment and the completeness of his case. Now if you were to object that a poem does indeed have a single particular meaning, namely that which the poet intended, and that its various readers simply make up some arbitrary meaning of their own, then I should reply that the form of the mirror is the form of the mirror maker. For was he not the first person whose face it reflected?[11]

These words of a Sufi master provide a perfect apologia for our anthology, both for the poems and the commentaries. We would not wish this book to be taken in any way as a final and definitive survey of Persian Sufi poetry, nor as an explanation of its meanings. Although we have tried to give a complete picture, it is still only one picture out of a great many possible. Sanā'i tells the story of the blind men and the elephant: One felt the trunk and declared, "Elephants are like ropes!" Another felt its leg and insisted, "Elephants are like great columns!" And so on. We hope that we have done better than this, but still we must insist that our collection, like a magic mirror, will inevitably show forth various "states and stations" to various readers.

Our chief purpose in choosing these particular poems was twofold: first, to offer a more-or-less complete "cycle of Sufism" through its literature, in such a way that enough major themes are represented to enable the reader to grasp something of this vast subject. Second, we chose poems that could be transformed into what we hope is good English poetry. Thus, we avoided poems that depend for their appeal solely or chiefly on their handling of the Persian language; and we avoided poems that depend on the reader's intimacy with Islamic history, theology, Koranic references, and the like. Instead, we concentrated on the essentials of content, unity of composition, and metaphor.

But we have several other secondary criteria for our selection. We wanted to offer a wide range of different types of poetry: not only lyrics (*ghazals*), but also odes (*qasidahs*), quatrains (*ruba'iyyat*), selections from longer narratives (generally *mathnawis*), mixed prose and poetry, didactic poems, fragments. Furthermore, we wanted to introduce new poets and lesser-known periods, so that along with famous authors such as Rumi, Hāfez, 'Attār, Sanā'i, Jāmi, and Nezāmi, we also looked for interesting pieces by authors famous as Sufis but not well known as poets, such as 'Ayn al-Qozāt Hamadāni and Ahmad Ghazāli. We have also included a number of very fine works by later poets of the Hindustani style, which has been sadly ignored ever since certain scholars pronounced it decadent.

Of course, in a culture like that of Persia, which is so firmly rooted in a poetic consciousness that one might well call it a bardic civilization, even the fifth-rate writers, the amateurs and poetasters, often come up with a few excellent pieces. In an anthology of this size, which moreover concerns itself with matters other than literary history in any comprehensive sense, many first-rate poets have been neglected. We never tried to include all schools, all regions, all periods, all genres, all major figures. That would have been an entirely different work (and a very valuable one, much needed). Nor have we included any of the verse written in traditional forms in the contemporary period—again, the subject of another possible book. This anthology does not represent the whole castle of Persian Sufi poetry, not even the door of the castle, not even the lock in the door. It is, however, a key to that lock.

We decided to produce this book because we realized that, for most English-speaking readers of poetry, the Sufi literature of Persia is indeed locked away behind massive doors of unfamiliar substance. Not even the clichés, not even the commonest tropes of this literature, much less its philosophic background, are known to the average, educated English or American reader. There is no point in going into the reasons for this incomprehension, nor in trying to fix blame for it. What is needed is a guide, an attempt to explain how to read Sufi poetry. Thus, this book.

For such a task, of course, one might choose any forty or fifty Sufi poems, almost at random. A good Sufi poem (say a *ghazal* from Rumi's *Divan-i Shams*)[12] may contain within its tiny form the whole of Sufi teaching. There are Sufi masters who expound all their doctrine and method through a relatively short work such as Shabestari's *Golshan-e rāz*. We have already explained why we chose the poems we chose, but it remains to admit to a certain arbitrariness (or perhaps we should say we were guided in part by our own "state of the moment and the completeness of our case"). In arranging the poems as they are presented here, we have followed only one out of a large number of possible sequences, based in part on a certain approach to Sufi philosophy or metaphysics, in part on traditional maps or outlines of the Path of the spiritual aspirant or traveler, and in part on literary criteria (variety, balance, unity of composition, etc.).

Thus, we begin with a poem on the nature of language itself, on the meaning of the Logos in Sufism. We then go on to reveal the emotions and thoughts of those seekers who become convinced that they are wasting their life and who desire to "wake up" and begin to follow the Path. Then, the short section called "The Secret" presents in miniature the whole philosophical justification for the belief that a Path in fact exists to be followed. "Awakening" outlines the methods of the Path. "Transcendence and Paradox" demonstrates the failure of human reason and conventional theology to answer the spiritual needs of the seeker.

The next four sections make up the heart of the book. They present the Path, and the doctrines of Sufism, in the symbolic terms of love, lover, and Beloved. This symbolism is the very essence of Persian Sufi poetry, and its imagery of eroticism and intoxication presents the chief barrier to a real understanding of the literature, as well as its chief charm and potency.

The last two sections, "Joy" and "The Perfect Man," present the culmination of the Sufi experience, the goal and end of the Path.

Each of the sections of the book represents a different facet of a world of symbolism, building up what we hope is a veritable palace of mirrors or a mosaic of light, capable of providing for the attentive reader a synthesis, an integral experience of Sufism. Words are not "the thing itself," true. But a poem, though made of words, is a kind of thing-in-itself, capable of touching the heart directly.

Yet the difference between Sufi poetry and other sorts of poetry cannot be said to lie exactly in its ability to touch the heart, since any good poem can do this. The reader will have no doubt, however, that in reading this book he has entered a different universe, a world whose inhabitants seem concerned with matters almost totally unrelated to worldly affairs. The wine they speak of does not seem to be available in bottles, and the beloved they praise sounds not quite human. These poets are indeed "Voices of the Unseen."

And yet for Western readers used to a clear distinction between "world" and "spirit," either excessively Aristotelian or excessively Platonizing, this Sufi poetry often seems irreligious and far from mystical. How can one speak of God in such *sensual* terms? Erotic emotion, wine, music, and the beauties of nature are all highly suspect in the post-Protestant world (a world with no religion, which still insists that religion be "out of this world"), yet these Persians seem to assume that such matters are essential to mystical literature.

These problems (and the fact that Persian poetry has found very few decent translators) bar too many readers from appreciating what is in fact one of the greatest of all spiritual and poetic realms, a universe still very much alive. Many of these poems are chanted in Sufi meetings or are known and loved by thousands of people who simply appreciate their beauty. If this book can unlock such a treasury and allow its readers some access to the philosophic, spiritual, or even merely cultural pleasures of the palace of Persian Sufi poetry, then we will echo the poets themselves, who always ended their books with:

AL-HAMDOLIL 'LĀH

Praise Belongs to Allah

NOTES

1. His famous *mathnawi, Hadiqat al-haqiqa*, has been partially translated into English. See the bio-bibliographies which follow the text.

2. Ahmad Ghazāli is the first and, so far as we know, the only one who has used this telling expression (in his *Sawāneh*).

3. The *Mishkat al-anwār*, translated by W. H. T. Gairdner (Lahore, 1952; 1st impression, London, 1924).

4. The first English translation of this seminal work, together with a commentary by Nasrollah Pourjavady, was published in 1986.

5. See S. H. Nasr, *Three Muslim Sages* (Cambridge, MA, 1969) for an introduction to the life and works of Sohrawardi.

6. See "The Last Will and Testament of Ibn 'Arabi's Foremost Disciple" by W. C. Chittick in *Sophia Perennis*, vol. 4, no. 1 (Spring 1978).

7. See *Heart's Witness: The Sufi Quatrains of Awhaduddin Kirmānī*, ed. with commentary by B. Manuel Weischer, trans. by Peter Lamborn Wilson and B. Manuel Weischer (Tehran, 1978). W. C. Chittick and P. L. Wilson have published a translation of 'Erāqi's *Lama'at* under the title *Divine Flashes* (New York, 1982).

8. See T. Izutsu, *Sufism and Taoism*, part 1 on Ibn 'Arabi (Tehran, 1979); *Creative Imagination in the Sufism of Ibn 'Arabi* by H. Corbin, trans. by R. Mannheim (Princeton, 1969); *Three Muslim Sages* by S. H. Nasr; *The Wisdom of the Prophets* by Ibn 'Arabi, trans. from the French of T. Burckhardt by A. Culme-Seymour (Aldsworth, 1975).

9. The *Tarjuman al-ashwaq*, trans. by R. A. Nicholson in 1911; new edition with an Introduction by Martin Lings (London, 1978).

10. See F. Schuon, *The Transcendent Unity of Religions* (New York, 1953).

11. 'Ayn al-Qozāt Hamadāni, *Nameha-ye 'Ayn al Qozāt* (Tehran, 1969), vol. 1, p. 216.

12. Several selections in translation exist; see the bio-bibliographies.

PROLOGUE

Helāli

ON THE LOGOS

Speech
is the preface
to the Book of Love,
treasury
of the King
of Love,
the bounty you seek
from the heart.
What have I said?
Whatever you say
is LOGOS,
ocean-fountain
pearl-hoard
incisive proof
of the Intellect
whose cutting edge
is but the blade of the tongue
which reveals the hidden fires
which sears the universe
with the heart's candle flame.

If the Word
were not painted on

the cosmic page
there would be no sign
of Adam or the world
no talk of past or future.
Who
could have kindled
mercy in the heart
of the thief
of hearts?
Who
could have made
Muslims out of infidels?
or made the minstrels
rejoice
or sparked a thousand flames
with a single breath?
LOGOS is Revelation
and we are the High Throne;
Speech is magic
and we are the enchanters.
Life
flows from eloquent speech:
where is there room
for the miracles of Jesus?
for with this breath
we enliven
a whole universe
and render it
everlasting.

At the beginning of his book *On the Attributes of Lovers*, Helāli justifies his own literary activity. Why, after all, should anyone say anything at all? His answer takes us into the realm of metaphysics. In Islam, Revelation takes the form of the Koran, which is Speech or Logos *(kalam)*. (In Christianity, it takes the form of Jesus himself, a man; but Jesus is also the Logos, both for Christianity and Islam, which knows him as *kalemat-al'llāh*, "the Word of God.") For esoteric Islam, the Book or Word ultimately refers to Creation as a whole, and thus to its central manifestation, the Perfect Man (e.g., Jesus, or Mohammad). But Logos precedes even Creation itself. The Day of Covenant, when God asked, "Am I not your Lord?" and man answered, "Yea, verily" (VII, *72)*,* took place in "pretemporality" *(azal)*. Thus, God's Word was heard before even His Face (i.e., His formal Self-manifestation) was seen.

*All references in parentheses are to the Koran. Translation is that of the authors.

LEAVING THIS WORLD BEHIND

Buddha founded his Path on the human fact of suffering. Islam gives the basic situation in which we find ourselves a slightly different interpretation: man in his ordinary state of consciousness is literally asleep ("and when he dies he wakes," as Mohammad said). He lives in a dream, whether of enjoyment or suffering—a phenomenal, illusory existence. Only his lower self is awake, his "carnal soul." Whether he feels so or not, he is miserable. But potentially the situation can be changed, for ultimately man is not identical with his lower self. (The Prince of Balkh, Ibrāhim Adham, lost in the desert while hunting, chased a magic stag, which turned on him and asked, "Were you born for this?") Man's authentic existence is in the Divine; he has a higher Self, which is true; he can attain felicity, even before death ("Die before you die," said the Prophet). The call comes: to flight, migration, a journey beyond the limitations of world and self.

Sarmad

QUATRAIN: LIFE'S ILLUSION

You sleep
you forget yourself
and forgetfulness

21

brings no fruit but regret.
Your friends have gone ahead
you too are on the way;
Why do you not contemplate
life's illusion?

Najmoddin Kobra

QUATRAIN

What never existed
leaves nothing in the hand
but wind
while "reality"
offers nothing but imperfection
and failure;
that being the case
one can only dream
of what never was
and as for what "really is,"
remember:
it doesn't exist.

The world in its separative sense is a world of becoming rather than being: things are, but then again, things are not. Nothing in this world can be permanent. You may dream that things which do not exist will come into being and that all your desires will be fulfilled, and yet all that you possess here and now is doomed to pass away. This being the case, man's mental experiences of this world are not real knowledge, which pertains only to being, but merely dreams and opinions.

Attār

THE HUMAN CASE

Do not boast when the wheel of fortune swings
you aloft; another twirl will land you on the bottom
mark.
The sun reaches the zenith and begins to descend:
so also falls the fool who follows it.
The human case is sealed in a talisman chest;
who has not been seared and blackened
with this pain?
Bound and trapped he utters no word except in
misery:
Wa! wound from crown to feet in loops of chain.
Who—like the green narcissus—has eyes to see the
world's way
shrivels and fades to escape being plucked
for the vase.
Narcissus with eyes of wisdom stoops low
in fear of death
while Cypress, free and tall, stands proud
in forgetfulness.
Fragile bloom with a necklace of thorns, life span less
than a week,
why do you forget your death and deck yourself
in gold?

Something has fallen like snow on the world
    of your face;
    rise from your bed of stupor and sadness:
    the caravan departs.
Death's dynasty will conquer, even after a century
    while you still clutch your seventy-odd years.
Did morning smile at you? Then be sure the day
    grows dark,
    for dawn only rose and grinned in mockery.
One camel in the caravan hears the bray of a desert ass
    and, frantic, yanks at the bridle to follow its voice.
You are that camel, the donkey's bray the noise
    of fame:
    you tug at the reins but at last must plod
    from Rome to Turkestan.
Your carnal soul is a cur, bitch stained with filth—
    but brave enough
    to hunt for lions if you train it like a lamb;
yet it plots to make peace with the wolf
    and cavorts like a trained goat to trick you.
Stick no rooster's crown on your ego in vanity and lust
    lest like the coronet of Iblis it bind you to
    your throne.
Behold the seeker who yearns for the absence of Truth:
    the universe wears a dervish cloak patched
    with heavens upon heavens.
Each month mounts a yellow stallion, sets out its
    first evening
    upon its path, the crescent moon its horseshoe.
But how soon the silver shoe falls beneath our horizon,

how quickly lifetimes ride away on racing steeds.
If the Cosmos cannot find what it desires on
    Resurrection Day
    it will tear through nine layers of curtains
    like silk robes
and ripping apart the gossamer of stars find
    what it seeks,
    cut the branch of desire, pluck up the roots of self.
Like the wheel of heaven, those who are veiled
    from themselves
    are veiled by their selves, heads spinning like
    proud galaxies.
Rend the veil from the face of your existence,
    flee calamity,
    drink the poison of death's hour, win the sweet juice
    of the cup.
The medicine for heart's pain is the death of your
    tarnished soul—only this:
    the homeopathic cure: a bit of poison.
You are the pearl of the world: sit silent in ocean's deep;
    do not strut the shore showing off to banks of
    worthless reeds.
In the ranks of heroes who can rival you? Why bother
    to set feet in stirrup, stretch hand to lasso?
Your foe like a vine leaf will turn yellow and fall;
    why plunge your fingers to the wrist in the wine
    of his blood?
Your heart, your eye, your soul are macrocosm and
    microcosm:
    who can equal you in this paltry universe?

Ranks of angels bow in the dust before you
burning wild rue to ward off the evil eye.
The archangel brings you the diamond of paradise:
why do you fling it in the mud?
Compared to you the Messiah is a kindergarten brat:
why do you waste your time on ancient texts?
So subtle and virgin
the thoughts of 'Attar,
what a pity he couldn't
make use of them all!
My God, the desires
of the ego have slain me,
ravaged me like
a disgusting disease.
But yet if it please Thee
then save me, my Lord
that desire may not make
Thy 'Attar a buffoon!

'Attār's ode presents in condensed imagery the whole basic Sufi view of man: limited to his "carnal soul" (*nafs-e ammārah*), he is the toy of fortune, here seen as a cosmic malevolence that calls to mind the Buddha's teaching on suffering. In his true self (his "soul at peace," *nafs-e motma'nnah*), however, he is the axis of Creation, the shadow of God on earth. The poet, therefore, attempts to awaken his reader's "blaming soul" (*nafs-e lawwamah*), the faculty by which one may discriminate the unreal from the Real and seek to advance toward what (in potentiality) one *already is.*

Sarmad

QUATRAIN: THE DEATH TRAP

*Each of your body's cells
is a type of death.
With one puff
your thorn-fire is blown out.
You are the victim
your case rests with the hunter
but struggle as you will
you'll find the death trap.*

Sanā'i

STALE LOAVES

*Forgetful heart
sleep not too much
in this wayside inn;
listen: the alarm:
get up, pack:
the caravan goes,
youth's day goes,
black hair
turns gray,
the messenger
of the end of Time
knocks: Saddle
your camel.
Your parents are dead*

27

your children abandon you,
nothing remains but an image
a feeling of loss:
get up, see
the graveyard outside
and consider
what skulls and vertebrae
and ribs lie scattered
under its dirt,
what curls
which framed
an oval face
are now become
ringlets of fire.

Do not lean
on the shifting world:
lions in caves
horses in wild herds
are brought to dust:
soon the hunchback sky
will collapse,
Saturn, Jupiter,
Leo, Virgo——
all shall fall,
your love of music
wine and excitement
evaporate.

You bought a house

laid out a garden
paid for the land
with usurious
investments,
built your walls
with profits
from your crops:
the carpet you tread
is woven of fine
dun satin
and the soft hair
of lambs,
while the hands
of the widow next door
are cracked
with blisters:
she sleeps hungry
while you gorge
your stomach,
fat as a cubic square,
a pregnant womb!
You bargain hard—
the whole ball of dough
or nothing—
but in Sacred Law
you can't tell
a monastery
from a garbage dump.

The thief holds up

29

travelers with his
sharp sword,
the merchant
with his thumb
upon the scales.
If you go one night
to the mosque
be sure
you walk with
bright torches
so everyone will note
your piety.

In the Holy Months
you eat orphans' money,
break your fast
like a snake
in a charmer's basket
on their stolen goods.
With orphans' money
you sit a
forty-day retreat:
Oh give back
what you have robbed
and quit your
hypocrite cell!

You've become
a model Sufi
hanging around

the doors of princes
and viziers:
they say dervishes
are allowed to carry
leftovers away
from banquets:
is that why you've made
your patchwork cloak
of wool?

When you eat
thank God,
when you starve
be patient:
don't bitch
to heaven
about daily bread.
How long will you run
oh my son
after stale loaves,
carrying assloads,
scuttling like a
hungry dog?
Clutch the sleeve
of Unity and listen
to Sana'i's advice
and on Resurrection Day
maybe you'll escape
the fires
of hell.

31

Sanā'i writes from within an atmosphere of Sufism, which leads him to criticize not only the hypocritical exoterist, but the false Sufi as well: all his satirical portraits are as up-to-date as a newspaper, not because they are topical, but because they are timeless. The style, however, is pure sermonizing (*maw'izah*), unlike the mere literary approach of 'Attār, and reminds us that many of the earlier Sufis (including, for example, 'Abd ol-Qader Gilāni and Ahmad Ghazāli)* preached from pulpits to a public by no means all esoterically inclined. The simple and potent (and humorous) approach to ethics in a poem like this would presumably appeal to the ordinary reader (or listener), but be read with pleasure by a mystic as well (or with displeasure, if he recognized himself in the caricature of the pseudodervish).

* 'Abd ol-Qāder Gilāni (died 562/1166) was the founder of the Qāderi Sufi order, today perhaps the most widespread in the world. For details on the life of Ahmad Ghazali, see the bio-bibliographies.

Bābā Afzal Kāshāni

QUATRAIN

My hearing, sight, my tongue and hand: all He.
Then I am not, for all that is, is He.
I think I am, and thought is but a dream.
When I awake, all that remains is He.

According to the Prophet, God says, "My servant

continually seeks to come near Me by means of works of supererogation, until I love him; and when I love him, then I am his hearing, his sight, his tongue, hand, foot, etc." In this statement, the duality of Lord and servant still shapes the actual structure of the sentence, but it is nevertheless clear that the servant possesses nothing of himself. His "existence," says Bābā Afzal, is but a dream. True existence belongs to the Lord, the One Who really sees, hears, and so on. Thus, the very act of "waking up" to the illusory quality of our ordinary state of consciousness already holds—potentially—the whole of the Path within it; although, to be sure, a great deal of "work" and "traveling" remains to be done before this potential can be fully realized.

33

THE SECRET:
THE FIRST MEETING

Take one step outside yourself:
The whole Path lasts no longer than a step.
—Shāh Ne'matollāh Wali

From God's "point of view," the Path is as much an illusion as the world itself. Man does not *become*, but rather already *is*, fully realized. His realization is in itself a metaphysical reality, true beyond all time and becoming. But this primordial fact, this secret of secrets, is obscured by Adam's forgetfulness and must be recovered through our own remembrance. There is nothing sinful, in the usual Christian sense, about this forgetfulness. Neither Nature nor man's nature is radically flawed by the Fall: the real Self is identical with the Divine. Our task is to recover that identity.

The doctrine of the Unity of Being is not simple pantheism, if we understand this to mean that God and the world are identical on the level of the world. But the concept of Unity must be taken to imply that the world and God are identical on the level of God. The difference between Creator and creation, Lord and servant, God and man, is a difference between two levels of the same Reality or Existence. Creation, as the relative, is interpreted as a manifestation of the Absolute. Creator and creation are thus *essentially* one. Man in his essence is already his own goal, potentially already the Perfect Man.

God is the source of every Positive thing in this world. Love, which permeates this world, is a manifestation of the Divine Attribute LOVE, and it is by virtue of this Divine Attraction that the world coheres. Everything is filled with Love, everything is intoxicated with this wine. We live in a drunken universe.

Among all beings in this universe, man holds a special privilege. He alone can fully realize Love, make love with the Beloved and become the mirror of His Attributes. This privilege was given to him when in Preeternity God made a Covenant with man: "Am I not your Lord?" Man answered, "Yea, verily we witness" (VII, 172). Thus the Divine Beauty was presented to man's spirit in the form of the Beloved, and from that timeless Time we are become lovers, trapped by Love's snares; for in accepting the Covenant, we were sealed or branded.

"After" this, man was sent to this world. From the Divine and Eternal, he fell into the human realm of temporality. We cannot claim that this is unjust. God Is All possibility, and the possibility of separation must be realized in creation. In fact, without the drama of loss and recovery, of God playing hide-and-seek with Himself, there could be no Mercy (which requires an object), no Love (which requires a lover). The Divine would then be imperfect—which is absurd.

So it is that we spend our time here suffering the

pain of Love, seeking ultimately nothing but to Return, to reawake in that "day" when we experienced Beauty in its totality.

The following poems give away this secret. The rest of the book concerns itself with all the aspects of the drama brought into play by that secret, the drama of yearning and nostalgia, work on the Self, loss and reunion.

Abu Sa'id Abo'l-Khayr

QUATRAIN

On Unity's Way:
no infidelity
no faith.
Take one step
away from yourself and—
behold!—the Path!
You, soul of the world,
must choose the road
of Divine Submission
then sit with anyone you like
—even a black snake—
but not your self!

Shamsoddin Maghrebi

THE GAME

Craftily my idol without you and me
somewhere eternally makes love with Himself
    a narcissist worshiping Himself night and day
    now the idol, now the idolater.
The whole of His essence curls itself up
into a tongue to speak about Himself:
    the Joseph of His beauty attires Himself
    in heaven and earth as brocade robes.
He hides Himself, peeks out from the collar
of the universe, adorns Himself with scarves of spirit
    and flesh;
    arrayed in gowns of body and soul He finds
    a thousand assemblies crowded with Himself,
draws up His armies on the field
throws the world into battle and strife:
    unrest and turmoil boil up from the planet
    as the army of His loveliness begins its charge.
From swirling clouds of black night the sun rises:
His face emerging from behind tangled curls,
    His cheeks, His lovelocks make riots break out
    in China, Tartary and Bulgaria.
Child, old man, young man, woman—all become
the place of manifestation of His beauty's sun:
    He speaks from every mouth, that the tale
    of His own adventure might reach His own ears.
When love sees His own beauty manifest

37

in the drapes and veils of "I" and "we"
jealousy flares up and He orders His beauty
"Rip from your limbs the clothes of
other-than-Me."
So He strips naked His beauty and resides
serene in His own essence:
When the tides of the ocean of Unity swell
the multiple universe is sucked back into Himself,

Then in that instant O Maghribi there will be
no other, nothing but essence, no space, no time.

Shamsoddin Maghrebi, "the Sun of the West," is greatly esteemed by Persian Sufis for the conciseness and pure gnostic clarity of his writings. A spiritual descendent of Ibn 'Arabi, he is almost always concerned with the central theme of Creation as the Self-manifestation of the Absolute; each of his poems is a complete exposition of this doctrine, each from a different point of view.

Here the original Unity, in love with Itself, manifests Itself as the realm of plurality; then, jealous of Itself, as it were, It calls everything back into Itself: "Everything perishes but His Face" (XXIIX, 88).

'Ayn al-Qozāt Hamadāni

FRAGMENT

Our friend
ran into the house

38

slammed the door tight
and hid himself!
Now if I come
and knock on the door
what a ruckus I'll raise
in that house!

Shāh Jahāngir Hāshemi

THE TALE OF THE UNIQUELY BEAUTIFUL MIRROR MAKER

There was an idol once (by which we mean
To say, a youth whose beauty could inspire
Idolatrous praise) who lived in Syria
And earned his keep by making mirrors in
The city of Aleppo. Sweet were his lips,
His mouth a rosebud, cheeks as fresh as rain
Upon the desert, and his face was called
The Mecca of true lovers. Like the vault of heaven
His eyebrows curved, or like two crescent moons.
The sun in shame before his loveliness
Drew close upon its face a veil of cloud
And at his kiss the Fount of Life might flow
From sterile rock. No one can tell, no pen
Of poet celebrate such perfect grace.

Now no one in Aleppo loved this youth
As much as he himself; so fond was he
Of his own beauty that he wished no bliss
But to admire himself unceasingly

39

As with a hundred eyes. So, to that end,
He set out to construct a palace which
Would be unique as he who planned to live
In it. All arts, of mason, architect
And carpenter, he orchestrated in
His work; but last and most important he
Himself set out with all his skill to make
The interior of his castle one vast hall
Of mirrors: every wall and ceiling,
Every inch of surface he contrived to coat
With magic glass backed by gold enamel
Far more lustrous than the light of sun
Or moon, each of the mirrors made of glass
Like gemstone varied as a rainbow, each
As clean and polished and reflective as
The finest Chinese import. To be brief,
His palace rivaled heaven. It was fine
And perfect as your sweetheart's eye when you
Yourself, the pupil of her beauty, see
Yourself reflected in its mirror'd depths.

The bright house was complete but empty still
Till he, the mirror maker, entered in
To view it—and himself. Ah, then the veil,
The curtain of sweet unity was torn
From the face of eternity. Ah, then
The companionship of the mirror-hearted ones
Began. His face, reflected in each glass
Found its own reflection in the next
And next and next. Then, and only then

Were his exquisite down, his beauty spot
At last revealed in all their purity
And grace. At last the beauty that he owned
Was finally unfolded to his sight
In every sweet detail . . . in ecstasy.

O Hashemi! This place of vision, like the sky,
Is nothing but the reflection in one place
Of one supreme and perfect Beauty. We
Are like mirrors of this mirror house
Gazing from Above as from Below
Like the eye grown simple. So be cut
Off from yourself, that the sun of His grace might shine
According to the polish of your soul.
For nothing but the One is to be seen
Reflecting to infinity in all
This carnival of mirrors, where the form
Of every glance is but the shadow of
That Form Divine, and all the world is but
The double of His Essence, Space, and Time
The Book wherein He writes His magic signs.
    And if our mirror has gone dark
    Our treacherous eyes grown dim with cloud
    It is our faults that veil the spark
    Of His perfection. Cry aloud
        O Hashemi
        Then woe is me!

This rather free translation of a poem by Sayyed
Shāh Jahāngir Hāshemi makes use of one of the

41

commonest symbols in Islamic poetry—the mirror. The creation of the world is likened to the construction of a house of mirrors (ā'inah khānah), a style of interior (and even exterior) decoration that may have begun in India, but reached its rather overwhelming peak in nineteenth-century Iran. Each little mirror reflects the Lord of the House, the Beloved (the Syrian youth), sometimes poetically called "the idol" (bot-buddha-or sanam). Each mirror is like a heart, which can reflect the Lord only if it has been polished or purified by gnosis. The reflected images are one in respect to that which is manifested in them, many in respect to the loci of manifestation. The youth's apparently excessive admiration of himself of course symbolizes the very purpose of Creation: God's beauty is only perfect if it is experienced—but in essence there is only God Himself, seer and Seen: "I was a Hidden Treasure and I wanted (or "loved") to be known. So I created the World so that I might be known" (a hadith Qodsi in which God speaks through the Prophet).

Salmān Sāvāji

THE DRUNKEN UNIVERSE

*In Preeternity
    already the reflection
        of your ruby wine
        colored*

the cup
already poor lovers
fell into raging
thirst—
Lip of the cup
crystaled with sugar
from your garnet lips,
the hidden secret
of the jug
poured out
into Everybody's
mouth—
Adam saw
the black mole
on your wheat-
colored
cheek:
tricked by the bait
he fell into
the snare—
Western wind
untied
the riband
of your hair
dark tresses
smothered your
luminous face
and the armies
of Islam
suffered a hundred defeats

43

at the hands
    of hordes
        of infidels—
            for lovers:
the first slip he pulled
    out of the hat
        was marked
            with my infamous
                name—
Love
    ripped open the curtain
        of puritanism
and revealed
    my desire
        for paradise—
My bathtub fell off
    the roof!
        who doesn't know me?
What's the point
    of banging my drum
        in the cellar?
Last night Salman
    was trying to write
        about Sorrow
fire dripped
    on the page
smoke rose
    from the tip
        of his pen.

Salmān, a poet much admired and even imitated by Hāfez, speaks here of the Self-manifestation of the Absolute in forms, forms that are at one and the same time traps and modes of liberation. Even "before Creation" (in the ontological sense, not as an event in Time), man is destined to captivity in the world of multiplicity; but at the same time he is destined for reunion, for return to the Origin. Hence the poet's sadness is metaphysical, not egoistic—although he fears his eccentric behavior has made him as conspicuous as if his bathtub had fallen off his roof with a crash!

"Wheat-colored cheek" refers to the Islamic version of Adam's fall, which involved not an apple, but a grain of wheat.

Mahmud Shabestari

THE SPILLED CUP

The Universe: His wine cellar;
the atom's heart: His measuring cup.
Intellect is drunk, earth drunk, sky drunk
heaven perplexed with Him, restlessly seeking,
Love in its heart, hoping at least
for a single whiff of the fragrance
of that wine, that clear wine the angels drank
from that immaterial pot, a sip of the dregs—
the rest poured out upon the dust:
one sip, and the Elements whirl in drunken dance
falling now into water, now in blazing fire.
And from the smell of that spilled cup
man rises from the dust and soars to heaven.

AWAKENING

Imprisoned in the cage of the world (the world in its negative, "worldly" sense, not in the positive sense of the world-as-icon or Divine Manifestation), man is exiled and forgetful of his true home. To keep his part of the Covenant, to be faithful to his promise, he must set out on the Path from sleep to awakening. It is only the blessed few for whom this Path lasts no longer than a single step, although in theory all that is needed is to "turn around" or "inside out" and *be* what one *is*. For most seekers the Path is long; one Sufi speaks of "a thousand and one" different stages.*

"Everything perishes save His Face"; the first step on the Path is to begin to contemplate the futility of the world of dust, the world in which one's lower self is doomed. The seeker must renounce it all, including his own self, and seek that which is Everlasting. He must travel from things to Nothing, from existence to Nonexistence.

How does one get lost on purpose? Our present state is one of forgetfulness toward the Divine—the true Self—and remembrance of worldly affairs and the lower self. The cure for this is a reversal: remembrance of the true Self, the Divine within, and forgetfulness toward everything else.

In Sufism the basic technique for this is invocation

*See *Kitab mashrab al-arvah va huva'l-mashhur bi-hazar u yak maqam* by M. Ruzbihan al-Baqli al-Shirazi (Istanbul, 1974).

or "remembrance" *(zekr)* of the Divine Name, which is mysteriously identical with the Divine Being. Through this discipline the fragments of our directionless minds are regathered, our outward impulse turned inward and concentrated. This is the act of a lover who thinks of nothing but his beloved.

The following poems express these ideas in general terms, dealing with them not in didactic detail, but in such a way as to turn the reader's mind toward the importance of the task. They are not instruction manuals, but poems about the sacred technique of Sufism.

Nezāmi

THE INSIGHTFUL INDIAN SAGE

*A Hindustani sage passed by
a perfumed garden, a tinseled landscape
or botanical display where each rose
girded its loins in a blood blush
like the horizon's lurid sundown sash
and ephemeral tulips slept out brief lives
in a pretty stupor. A prism of flowers,
of wine mixed with too much sugar,
of blooms wounded with their own stamens
like shields stuck with arrows,
willows crepitating with a summer's fear,
violets strangling in the noose
of their own tresses. The eyes
of the narcissus fallen on their own skirts*

like a shower of drachmae. The tulip
necklaced with a rope of pearls,
the rose a touchstone for the turquoise—
lasting one day, lasting one breath.
No one is given more than a sigh,
no one ponders the consequences.
And the old man passed by.

Some months later he walked
that way again, and where
the nightingale had chanted he heard
the harsh whimper of swift sparrows,
the crow's rattle. Hell had crept
between the cracks of paradise—
the elegant Caesar of that palace
exiled to a gray suburban synagogue.
Greenness dissolved in steam,
the armload of blossoms now
a beggar's backload of thistles.
"How quickly they fly" he muttered
and laughed at them all and wept
for himself. "At their birth
they have no mind for mortality.
Anything that sticks its head up
out of the dust will be swept
to destruction. Nowhere is better
than the ruins, nowhere better
to turn my face."
                    This sage
sees with the eye of divine succor,

48

comes to know himself and so
to know God, becomes the banker
of a secret pearl and turns backward
all the way to nothingness toward the gem.

You my readers who think yourselves Muslims
though you haven't the virtues
of the Zoroastrians——like a fountain
which has not enjoyed one tear of rain——
never sink lower than my Hindustani sage:
renounce the world and tell it
"Cease to be." How long will you
puff yourselves like flowers, adorned
with cap and sash? Get up and leave
the rose's vampiric embrace:
this sash, this cap are Love's foes——
pawn them and buy passage to
Love's tavern of self-ruin.
The cap gives lordship over
this realm of clay. The sash
is slavery to your soul's desires ...

but liberate yourselves alike from slavery
and lordship——or free yourself like Nezami
from Nezami.

Characterized by Nezāmi's usual brilliant elegance, this is a profound and unusual poem, remarkable for the dark intensity with which the usually cheerful nature imagery of Persian poetry is metamorphosed by ascetic vision into disgust. From the exoteric point of view, the other religions were true, but are now abrogated or superceded by Islam; from the esoteric point of view they are not invalid, but, like pieces from an ancient mosaic embedded in the illusive and crystalline geometric tilework of a new mosque, their teachings are reworked and reborn, as it were, in an Islamic setting. The vision of the Hindustani sage (the actual word is *mawbad*, a Zoroastrian priest; Nezāmi may have meant him to be a Parsi) is not ascetic in the narrow or exoteric sense. Through the contemplation of nature in its aspect of *maya*, he is "ruined"*(khar āb)*, he dies to himself and goes toward "nothingness," the Nonbeing that he has perceived in the garden, his true end.

Ayn al-Qozāt Hamadāni

FRAGMENT

Nonexistence
within existence
is my Rule
getting lost
in getting lost
my Religion.

Sanā'i

INVOCATION

*New falconer
    teach heart's hawk
        the hunt of Thought
teach
    tongue's nightingale
        to invoke the Name;
the tongue
    (that fish
        in the mouth's fountain)
will relish the taste
    of divine
        remembrance.
Heart's theriac:
    to repeat and repeat
        "There is no God but He"
——but the heart
    must remain awake——otherwise
        it's nothing but hullabaloo.
Foster the spirit
    with remembrance——only then
        the heart finds peace in the Name,
His Name
    written in the
        Book of Unity,
the eternal
    Alchemy
        of Happiness.*

51

Invocation *(zekr)* is the central technique of Sufism, as it is of Hesychastic Christianity, Hinduism, and most schools of Mahayana Buddhism. The author touches not only on its exterior aspect—i.e., its actual practice—but also its esoteric meaning. Metaphysically, the practice of invocation is based on the mystery of the identity of God and His Name ("in the beginning was the Word"); in terms of spiritual practice, *zekr* is food for the tongue and nourishment for the heart: when the tongue mentions His Name and the heart remembers, or listens, and becomes aware, the invoker finds his highest satisfaction and peace. "Verily in the remembrance of Allah do hearts find rest" (XIII, 28; Pickthall's translation).

Sanā'i

MEDITATION

*Collect your mind's fragments
that you may fill yourself
bit by bit with Meaning:
the slave who meditates
the mysteries of Creation
for sixty minutes
gains more merit
than from sixty years
of fasting and prayer.
Meditation:
high-soaring hawk*

of Intellect's wrist
resting at last
on the flowering branch
of the Heart:
this world and the next
are hidden beneath
its folded wing.
Now perched before
the mud hut
which is Earth
now clasping with its talons
a branch of the Tree
of Paradise
soaring here
striking there——each moment
fresh prey
gobbling a mouthful of moonlight
wheeling away
beyond the sun
darting between the Great Wheel's
star-set spokes, it rips to shreds
the Footstool and Throne
a Pigeon's feather
in its beak——
or a comet——
till finally free of everything
it alights, silent
on a topmost bough.
Hunting is king's sport,
not just anyone's

53

pastime
but you?
you've hooded the falcon
—what can I say?—
clipped its pinions
broken its wings ...
alas.

In this comprehensive introduction to the practice of meditation, each image reflects precisely a technique or its result. Human thought, ordinarily fragmented and directionless, can be collected and organized; based on the Intellect, the purposeful center, it can soar through a fabulous cosmography (reminiscent of Taoist visions) and finally, rising above all imagery, attain to the freedom of silence. Such directed thought, or meditation, aspires to something higher than itself: Meaning (*ma'na*), supraformal or inner Reality. This is the topmost bough of the Paradise of the Presence, reached by the mind's hawk.

Shāh Dā'i Shirāzi

EXHORTATION TO AN EXPEDITION TO THE INTERIOR

Late one night I spoke with Meditation as if
it were a person: "O sea diver, what
rare pearl have you found to keep you so long
in heart's fathoms; in what darkness still

54

that corrodes the humors, what midnight deep
that rusts and cracks the intellect? How long,
    my Joseph
in this coal hole? My Jonah, how long in whale's gut?
Come out: all earth is an Egypt to that
bold pauper who unfurls a royal standard,
all the sky a throne in the grasp of an ambition
to soar. If your heart yearns for Khezr
the very dust will spring with immortal fountains;
if you want to be Moses, any walking stick
will writhe before you in serpentine coils. Come out!
The rose's smile unfolds in a perfumed garden,
the green grass preens itself in pride,
heaven's in festival, the fixed stars its guests,
the Zodiac sphere overturned and filled with wine;
the sun is a boy to pour, the moon beaming
like a jovial host. Stars pavane with tapers
in their hands till Dawn the bride tosses aside
night's tresses. What forms! From every corner
a handsome Joseph, a love-struck Zulayka:
the cypress envies this one, Reason totters,
the moon is jealous of that one, the Soul
staggers with love. Such an exquisite cosmos!
Come out for an hour and leave your
submarine wanderings. Time's Beginning and End
have wed and given birth to an Instant
which is cash in your hand. How long will you
run with the wind? Come and enjoy the world
and its soul pleasures; have mercy on your heart
if not on yourself!"

When Meditation
heard these words pour from my soul
it answered within my heart: "*Whore!*
Layabout! Slave of the carnal self! Know that
my station is given by God the judge—but yours
is subterranean. You think your little world
a universal, you think that Meditation is but
part of the whole—what mundanity!
What bad taste! What stupidity! Know that
here in Meditation the whole Universe is contained;
Life, Intellect, Soul ... all are here! My portion
is the Essence of Wisdom—yours the paintings
on a bathhouse wall. Here where I am
the angels rejoice, heaven is on display
while you keep watch by night ... with trolls.
"Come out!" you say. But I tell you, Come in,
ascend to this high threshold—leave the gutter—
this threshold which makes heaven and earth appear
but a pair of molecules, this vast space
where the sun itself seems but a tiny beast.
Come to this steppe where the trees of paradise
are planted, to this sea where pearls are born,
to that drunkenness which erases He and Thou,
to that Being which has swallowed I and We,
to that wealth which makes Haroun al-Rashid's vizier
look a beggar, to that generosity which makes
Hatam al-Ta'i seem miserly. Come to that Book
where Adam read the Names, and Creation found
the secret reason for its being named.
Be quick—one instant—plunging toward the heart—

and this is paradise. Prepare yourself—one instant—
for the heart's true labor: this is immortality. "

Meditation told me then: "I have made an allusion.
If you are a man of symbolic sense, you'll grasp
what I mean. Origin and End, Exoteric and Esoteric—
all this you'll understand, and cease to pollute
your inner eye with random imagery. Master,
you have shrunk yourself to an atom—but
you are the very Sun; you call yourself an earwig
but you are a Phoenix! You do not know
your own beauty and perfection, you labor
in grief and affliction. You run about
seeking an imaginary mouthful—don't be bitter
if I tell you: the sweetmeat is you!
Your fancy drags you to the Void, you roll
like a dog in the dust, while the Fountain of Life
is within you. Vagabond of the highway,
listen: you are the very Wheel of Heaven.
You seek the profane Stone—no wonder you burn
like silver in the crucible. You seek a phantom—
no wonder your face grows jaundiced as fool's gold.

"Come then, here is world upon world, and all
that you seek and desire. You yourself are the traveler
and the Goal, lover and Beloved. The earth
seems a riddle, but you—if you see yourself
with Love's eye—are the answer. All, all
subsists in the Unity of the Essence—but
you are too cross-eyed to see it straight;

everything is bathed in your light—but
you are blind. Low and high, I have seen it all
and know: You yourself are the Secret Essence. "

Where the previous poems speak in general terms of meditation, Shāh Dā'i here discusses specifically the contemplation of inner reality. In Sanā'i's verses, the "movement" of the poem is from the non-contemplative, fragmented mind to the contemplative, Self-centered mind; the action takes place within a single subject: the poet himself, who castigates his reader for "hooding the falcon." Shāh Dā'i's action also takes place within a single subject, who has already directed his thought, already learned something about meditation, but wishes to turn his powers out toward the world—rather like a "black magician"—to the attainment of potency and pleasure. Meditation is personified and speaks to the subject, castigating him for his error and suggesting a movement toward the "interior."

Like all the poems in this section, Shāh Dā'i's might be mistaken for an attack on nature. But the Koranic—and therefore the Sufi—view of Reality is unitive and hierarchical, and hence symbolic. Nature consists of "waymarks" or symbols. On its own level it is "real," but for the "eye of discernment" it points beyond itself to the supranatural, the Inward *(bāten)*. If Sufism sometimes seems indifferent to nature, it is because it seeks to break the bonds of a false naturalism and reach through spiritual hermeneutic *(ta'wil)* toward the Real.

Once someone found Rābi'ah* secluded in her hut, in a state of meditation, and asked, "Why don't you come out and contemplate the Creation?" She replied, "Why don't you come *in* and contemplate the Creator?" Creation, the Outer *(zāher)*, and knowledge of nature, must be transcended—and this is accomplished through meditation. One is almost tempted to see in this poem a dialogue between the Western and the Oriental mind, the one focusing its attention through experimental knowledge, the other through sapiential knowledge; the former finally breaking down, in its search for the "profane Stone," into materialism; the latter fixed steadfastly on Unity through Self-knowledge.

*The early woman saint of Basra (died 185/801). See M. Smith, *Rābi'a the Mystic and Her Fellow Saints in Islam* (New York: Rainbow Bridge, 1977).

Hāfez

THE VAGABOND HEART

*Happy the heart which avoids
a certain tourism of the soul
and does not enter in by every door
where someone beckons.
    It would be better
    not to desire your lips*

but how can the blackfly
not buzz the candy shop?
Do not make me wash
the pupil from my eyes with tears:
your beauty spot imprinted
on my sight indelibly.
    Do not withhold your perfume
from me like a zephyr becalmed
for without your musky tress
I cannot live on.
Do not be a gadabout
nor gawking vagabond, my heart;
there is nothing to be gained
by such a skill.
    Why do you disdain me
for a drunkard? Do you think
the Holy Law will fall into disrepute
from my paltry sins?
I the beggar desire a friend
with a body like the cypress
but no hand empty of silver and gold
will reach to embrace her waist.
    I see no one whose book of deeds
is black as mine. Why then
unlike the reed pen does the lampblack
of my heart not stain my head?
Do not try to seduce me from the Path
with a hoopoe's crown. Like a king
the white falcon does not bury its claws
in lesser prey.

60

Bring wine, and
(providing not a whisper
goes beyond this door)
serve Hafez before the rest!

Hāfez extends to himself an "invitation to
one-pointed concentration." He is a lover telling himself
to care for nothing but his Beloved, justifying this to
himself as the one worthwhile occupation. He asks for
help from the Beloved herself, just as the Sufi sees his
own spiritual activity dependent for its success on Divine
Grace. Finally, he refuses all temptations to disperse
himself, and like one who practices meditation, he shuts
the doors of his senses, the better to savor the inner
intoxication of his contemplation.

'Ayn Al-Qozāt Hamadāni

QUATRAIN

Within the eye of the eye
I placed an eye
polished and adorned
with her beauty
but suddenly fell
into the Quarter of Perfection
and now am freed from sight,
from even the eye of contemplation.

TRANSCENDENCE
AND PARADOX

From the very beginning of his Path-faring, the traveler is faced with one vast and seemingly unbearable paradox: the "place" where he wants to go is "nowhere" (*nā-kojā-ābād*). We may know, intellectually at least, that our true self and the Divine Self are one. We may have faith that this is so. But faced with our own nothingness, we are overwhelmed by the foolhardiness of our undertaking. God, after all, is God, and we are but servants—yet even this presumes too much. How do we dare ascribe to ourselves a relationship with God? Say rather: the Absolute in its absoluteness cannot be known.

'Attār

IMPOSSIBLE

Invisible:
*   how can I see your face*
untouched
*   wrapped in yourself?*
Who
*   will show me the way?*
*   You have no homeland ...*
Who
*   will tell me news of one*
*   beyond all speech?*

Who are you
Lord, soul, boundlessly perfect;
how
can I describe the indescribable?
Never
a jewel bought or sold
more perfect than you:
ocean
cannot contain you nor
have you risen from its deep . . .
Why
do you sit in your pavilion
destroying
those who love but cannot enter
overwhelming
conquering the soul?

I knock on the heart's door
but you do not come out.
'Attar offers you his life
but you will not come
to collect it.

Divinity in Its Transcendence, the Absolute before any Self-manifestation, cannot be contemplated, for contemplation implies a subject and an object, and the Absolute is beyond all duality, all "place" and all knowing. It is the Mystery, the utterly inscrutable secret in the deepest part of Being, veiled behind all the inmost veils, yet somehow luring and teasing the lover. And the lover waits outside the door, ready to surrender his life at a sign.

'Ayn al-Qozāt Hamadāni

FRAGMENT

I know:
    there where you are
I cannot come;
    I know:
here where I am
    you will not come;
I know.

SEPARATION AND SADNESS

Like a lover who is spurned by his Beloved, the seeker now finds himself wandering in a strange desert, exiled forever from his former comfortable state of ignorance, but seemingly banished as well from the Presence he so desires. By the very "taste" of his love, he has already attained a measure of certainty: he *knows* the Beloved exists—he may even have caught a glimpse of her. But can he reach her?

Hāfez

LETTER TO THE SHAYKH OF JĀM

Sufi, approach and see the clarity of this jeweled vintage
    in the burnished looking glass of the cup.
Beg the secret from those profligates behind the curtain:
    not the puritan, but only he of high Station
    attains this State.
Fold up your nets and go—no one hunts the Phoenix—
    the trap's hand holds nothing but empty wind.
At the banquet of the Age take one cup, two cups
    and go. No more than this. No perpetual Union.
My heart, youth drains away and you've not plucked
    one rose:
    Don't be an old laughingstock! It's not too late to
    start now!
Carpe diem, for when the fountainhead dried up
    even Adam fled the garden of the Abode of Peace.

As for us at your threshold, at your command
my master, look with pity on your servants;

(signed) Hafez, disciple of Jamshid's Cup.
Now vagrant breeze, go and take
these signs of servitude to the Shaykh of Jam.

This is a sort of spiritual letter to a long-dead shaykh and poet, Ahmad-e Jām (see the bio-bibliographies). In it Hāfez complains that God in His Essence cannot be contemplated—but when he manifests Himself or takes the form of the Beloved, then the seeker, the lover, sees His Face in the mirror of the heart and becomes intoxicated by this unveiling. As long as he retains his individual identity as a lover (even though this is in itself a "high Station"), this state of intoxication is the most he can hope to attain. Some Sufis have said—though they are not always consistent in this—that no one *in this life* can go higher; in any case, if the seeker desires "perpetual Union" he must lose all identity in the One and cease, in a sense, to be even a lover. This is the ontological level of the Essence, which is symbolized by Hāfez (and other poets) by the *Simorgh,* a fabulous bird here (rather inadequately) translated as "Phoenix." If—or since—this goal cannot be attained in this life, the Sufi should still value the state of contemplation of the Beloved, for even though it does not last, it is the only worthwhile end in life.

(Perhaps a defense of the deliberate

Elizabethan–Jacobean echoes in this translation is in order. The Neoplatonic doctrine, that one reaches to the Essence through forms, even through the pleasure taken in beauty, was probably more widespread in English Renaissance poetry than present-day scholarship would admit. The *carpe diem* poetry of a Suckling or Lovelace must be understood at least partially in this light, even if the mysticism that animated a Drayton, or even a Shakespeare, was by then only dimly recalled. One feels that Hāfez would have read it in such a light!)

'Ayn al-Qozāt Hamadāni

QUATRAIN: FORBIDDEN HAREM

If in their weakness my legs
do not run after you, never think
it's because my heart is not caught
in your love;
> *it's not the case*
that I hold back because
I'm not your customer
>> *—only*
my eye is forbidden
the harem
of your Vision.

'Ayn al-Qozāt Hamadāni

QUATRAIN: A DOOR KNOCKER

In my dream all of me
is with her: lip upon lip
breast to breast

I whisper: "My heart,
would this night might last
forever . . ."

I wake and find myself
like a door knocker ...
hanging outside.

Helāli

MY MADNESS, YOUR BEAUTY

Heartless ones have no sorrow
but a worldly malaise
while in the grief of love
I have "lost touch
with world events."
Why knead Adam's clay
if not for love?
Those who have not become dust
in Love's Way
are less than human.
Now they are whispering

of my madness
and your beauty: the tale
could sell as well
as Layla & Majnun!
You branded me, and the doctor
with a "tsk tsk" tries
to pour salve on the wound—
I refuse! What flows from the sore
is the medicine I seek.
A bilious melancholic neurosis
makes me forget myself
and lose interest in the "outside world"
—or whatever it was
I once cared about.
Today your "life-giving breath"
has killed me at last;
what do I want with the
"healing breath of Jesus"
when I have such a death?
Well, don't expect any vulgar blooming buds
from the dust of Helali.
In his bleak garden
no room remains
for a cheerful heart.

The "healing breath of Jesus" refers to the Islamic belief that Christ, as the embodied Spirit (or "breath") of God *(ruh Allāh)* could breathe life into inanimate objects, such as clay birds, or revive the dead.

Layla and Majnun are the archetypal lovers of

69

Islamic literature (the most popular version of their story is by Nezāmi; see the bio-bibliographies).

Helāli treats these and other tropes—or clichés—of Sufi poetry with an unusual irony.

Helāli

THE CRESCENT MOON

Dawn:
 you rise from your chair
  and the rays from your face
   embroider the universe;
more graceful than the cypress
 or the rose—my God!
  what is this subtlety,
   this finesse?
Whatever you command,
 death or sorrow ...
  whatever you say
   whatever you want ...
Are you a soul
 that comes and goes so quickly?
  Are you a life, that leaves
   and does not return?
You sleep
 curled into yourself.... How I want
  your petal'd eyes this morning
   to fall first on me.
My heart

in separation, in loneliness
(what a fine affliction!) cries
for justice ...
Helali
scans the horizon every night
waiting for you like a crescent moon
to rise above the roofs.

The Absolute, in manifesting itself, is like the sun (as in Plato), which with its rays seems to bring all things into being from night's nonexistence. The world becomes the locus of manifestation of the Absolute. The Beloved (or God in the "creative imagination" of the worshiper) is but the mirror image, the icon of that original supraformal Reality. Only man, in his loneliness, can observe this image with true understanding; in the night of separation he waits for this image, the moon, to appear (helāl means "crescent moon"; the author plays with his pen name). He will thus prepare himself for the return, the final Union that comes about at the moment of his extinction and that is prefigured in the self-naughting of his love.

'Ayn al-Qozāt Hamadāni

FRAGMENT

0 would that the eye
had never seen
her face

71

that the heart
had never shared
the sin
of the eye!

LOVE AND THE LOVER

What is the nature of this Love in which the seeker now finds himself immersed? The Sufis say that the lover's "state" is always changing. We have seen him in his state of separation, nostalgia, "noble sadness." In the following section we have grouped together a number of poems, without implying any strict sequence or "spiritual progress," in which the lover's states are matched with degrees of knowledge. Thus, some of the poems are, so to speak, subjective and deal with the poets' perceptions of their condition. Others are more objective and describe through symbol and allegory the metaphysical truths realized by the lover in his voyage toward his goal.

Rābi'ah bent Ka'b

THE WILD HORSE

Again trapped
chained by
his love
all struggle
to escape
vain.
   Love
an ocean
with invisible
shores,

with
no shores.
If you
are wise
you will
not swim
in it.
To reach
the end
of love
you must
suffer many
unpleasantries
and think
it good,
drink poison
and find
it sweet.
I acted
like a
wild horse
not knowing:
to struggle
draws the
noose tighter.

'Ayn al-Qozāt Hamadāni

Quatrain: The Eternal Thirst

Long as I live I'll eat and drink
the sorrow of loving you
nor will I surrender it, this sorrow
to anyone when I am dead.
Tomorrow
when Resurrection comes
I'll walk forth with this raging thirst
still in my head.

Gharib Nawāz

Make Way for the King!

From spacelessness
love
descends
to lover's heart;
so sweep
yourself
up
for the King of the world
descends
to this dust heap
and
the soul

75

becomes as flesh
when the Soul of soul
plunges
into the soul
and why not?
If treasure
is dug in ruins
why not
love
in your heart?
Get out of the doorway!
the King of Love
approaches
the house:

All you nobodies
Out!
the guardian
of those
who have no one
approaches
the house
and
once the house
is vacant
of others
the mercy
will
descend ...

A King is lurking
in my closet
but the whole world
cannot contain him.
Once he gets here
both worlds
will implode
into dust
and
atoms——
for he
descends
no where
but
Nowhere.

What is the heart?
the hawk
of
High
Holy Heaven.
How can it bear
to nest
in the
herebelow?

Mo'in
is dust on the stoop ...

77

where else
would you expect
*to find him?**

Love in its essence is from Eternity, beyond Time and Space. Like a king from a holy land, it rides forth and in its journey descends for a while—perhaps for only an instant ("a breath")—into the world of duration and extension. Not just any "place" can receive the royal visitor however. Only in the heart can He reside, for the heart is the center, the function of which is to love. If the heart is occupied with the self, it is not functioning properly: it is idle. In order to "work" it must suppress all egoism. Paradoxically, when the king descends, He must reside in a "ruin," a heart destroyed to itself and empty.

*Mo'in is the poet's pen name.

Forughi

LOVER'S CRAFT

Again and again I polished my eye—now look:
it's become such a mirror that with a single glance
I can make you fall in love with yourself. Now look,
look deep into this glass and be aware
of other worlds.
　　　　　Now like a drunken reveler
pass by the monastery and the mosque:
you will be worshiped as the niche for prayer

by Muslim and Christian alike. Some night
    I'll strip the veil
from your face and you'll become Sun of the Kaaba,
Moon of the Church.
            If your braided tresses fell
in my hands I could forge a thousand chains for your feet;
if they gave me the Trees of Paradise on Judgment Day
I'd trade them both to ransom one rare embrace.

In Love's atelier my craftsmanship
reaches an unearthly beauty when
I contemplate your face.
            The whole world knows
I am a reprobate in love—but God forbid
I ruin your reputation as well, my love.

In these lines from Forughi's most famous poem, a
sort of serenade or song of lover to Beloved, the poet
claims that, although his Beloved is self-sufficient,
paradoxically she needs the love of the lover as the
mirror, the locus of her manifestation. He says he is
willing to polish the mirror so completely that nothing
remains of himself, so that the reflection will be perfect,
her face manifested totally therein.

'Attār

THE DULLARD SAGE

Lost in myself
 I reappeared
  I know not where
a drop that rose
 from the sea and fell
  and dissolved again;
a shadow
 that stretched itself out
  at dawn,
when the sun
 reached noon
  I disappeared.
I have no news
 of my coming
  or passing away—
the whole thing
 happened quicker
  than a breath;
ask no questions
 of the moth.
  In the candle flame
of his face
 I have forgotten
  all the answers.
In the way of love
 there must be knowledge

and ignorance
so I have become
both a dullard
and a sage;
one must be
an eye and yet
not see
so I am blind
and yet I still
perceive,
Dust
be on my head
if I can say
where I
in bewilderment
have wandered:
'Attar
watched his heart
transcend both worlds
and under its shadow
now is gone mad
with love.

In one sense, the Path is a radical unknowing, a
stripping away of all received certainties. Here 'Attār
explains that such unknowing is not the same as
ignorance, but is rather a state of purified consciousness
that leaves behind both knowledge and ignorance and,
paradoxically, reduces them to the same thing. In fact,
from the point of view of such a consciousness, all

81

dualities are confounded: seeing and blindness, for example. This is the utmost degree of awareness.

'Attar's image of the sun seems to go Plato one better. Thus the sun reaches its zenith: Reality at its most transcendent and yet, at the same time, most immanent. The seeker loses his separative existence, his "shadow," and at the same time is bathed in light. The drop of rain knows who and what it is as long as it remains a drop. When it falls back into the sea, its origin, it can no longer know. From the point of view of the "world," there is no way to describe 'Attār anymore—so he must be called "mad."

PASSING AWAY

Out of his gradually ripening experience of Love, the lover comes to realize that the Beloved, the Goal, cannot be reached as long as he remains locked into the world of opposites, as long as he himself remains himself. Rumi tells the story of a man who knocks at a door.

"Who's there?" asks a voice from within.

"It's me," says the man.

"Go away then," answers the voice. "There's no room here for 'me.'"

The man goes away and wanders in the desert until he realizes his error. He returns and knocks again at the door.

"Who's there?" asks the voice.

"Thou," answers the man.

"Then come in," the voice replies.

Sanā'i

MYSTIC CHAT

My dear!
You haven't the feet
for this path—
why struggle?
You've no idea where

83

the idol's to be found—
what's all this
mystic chat?
What can be done
with quarrelsome
fellow travelers,
boastful
marketplace
morons?
If you were really a lover
you'd see that faith and infidelity
are one ...
Oh, what's the use?
nit-picking
about such things
is a hobby for
numb brains.
You are pure spirit
but imagine yourself a corpse!
pure water which thinks
it's the pot!
Everything you want
must be searched for—
except the Friend.
If you don't find *Him*
you'll never
be able
to start
to even
look.

84

Yes,
you can be sure:
You are not Him—
unless
you can remove yourself
from between
yourself
and Him—
in which case
you
are
Him.

Nasimi

CANCELED OUT

Dawn:
the tavern:
I learned the inside way
from a licensed guide.

Old Man Love:
"Come in, come in:
don't loiter around
outside!"
Inside:
SPLENDOR
cups of pain.

85

The saki:
"Drink, drink!"
and he embraced me
tight
so close ...

SAKI/ME
both one
or one disguised
as two?
NOW WITNESS
NOW OBJECT-OF-SIGHT
NOW SAKI
NOW CUP ...
Nothing remains:
I know nothing:
all HIM
Nasimi: canceled out
in the beauty
of the
seducer.

In these two poems the same thing is described from two different points of view, or rather in two different modes. Sanā'i, who was known as a Hakim (gnostic/philosopher), discusses the difficulties of the Path and the conditions for entering the Tavern. He does not actually describe what will happen there; in fact, he is primarily concerned with criticizing the inadequacy of those who lack true understanding. Nasimi, however, enters the Tavern, drinks, and loses himself in Union. He emphasizes that this is not a process of two *becoming* one, but simply the cancellation, the nullification of one, that One may remain. While Sanā'i writes from the state of sobriety, Nasimi writes as one intoxicated. The first *depicts,* the second *experiences.*

Sā'eb Tabrizi

THE COMPASS

A Joseph will he be
who buys you
for a slave
a Jesus
who becomes
your patient.
The eye that thirsts
for your face will be singed
in the heart's sun spring:
grave candles of love-burnt seekers
flash in the night
like summer lightning.
Drowsiness in the shade
beneath your mud wall
is better than waking;
each space between the bars
of your prison cell
is an avenue to heaven
—how fortunate

he who falls
into your trap:
Resurrection's fearful floods
are but waves of a mirage
to your stupified lovers.
O if Sa'eb
could emerge from himself
circles of the galaxies
would seem no more
than the single point
of your twirling compass.

Sā'eb knows "where to go" but (in this poem at any rate) he hasn't "reached it." He knows Love's miracles, knows that true freedom lies in submission to the Beloved's will, that the cure lies in suffering for Love, that true existence lies in the extinction of the limited self, etc.—but for him this remains "speculative" rather than "experiential" knowledge, a nostalgia, not an accomplishment.

Forughi Bastāmi

MIDNIGHT SUN

A barfly like me
dead to himself
never spends a worry
on Reckoning Day.
If your work is mercy

then what is sin?
Good deeds? Where's the gain?
Nothing I do measures up
to your justice.

The tale of Hell
is but wind in my ear
so long as I'm cooked
on Separation's coals;
dawn's smoldering sighs,
night's tears testify
that your face, your hair
wash me in alternate
waves of fire and water.

All this desert's panthers
have fallen my prey;
the timid gazelle in your eye
calls me her brave cur.
Love makes me caper
before this mad parade
so long as my deflated
heart holds fast in the
chains of your hair.

Your black-drunk eyes
touch me in turbulent dream:
water falls from your lashes
and rousts me from sleep.
Now, saki, drown me
in an ocean of wine

before my thin barque's
caught and broken
on the Wheel of Time.
I blush before this
charming cupbearer
till cup after cup
wash away Shame's veil;
I boast that even at night
I see the Sun's fountain;
"Yes," he agrees,
"—so long as someone unties
the blindfold from your face!"

Forughi! I cry out
in the pain of a tight-tied breast
but from those sweet lips
comes never reply.

To attain Union with the Beloved (symbolized here, among other images, by the Midnight Sun), the lover must die to himself, to his self. This self-annihilation is called *fanā* in Arabic; the Persian poets often use the terms *kharābi*, ruin, and *kharābāt*, the state or station of being ruined. *Kharābāt* is also used to mean a tavern and thus, by allegory, the *khāneqāh* or Sufi meeting place. The man of *kharābāt* is one who has cut all attachments to world and self and has become intoxicated with Love. He can claim to think nothing either of this world or the next, neither of punishment nor reward. Concerned only with the Beloved, he lives in expectation of His justice and Mercy and holds Him responsible for his own fate, his happiness and sorrow, his suffering, his Union and Separation. All comes from the Beloved, because he has lost his self in His Self.

Sarmad

QUATRAIN: MY SINS

My Sins
and the Friend's forgiveness:
I cannot begin
to figure up
an account
that has no end.
Forget this
tormenting guilt
over your misdeeds:
His Eye of Mercy
loves the beauty
of sin.

The spiritual traveler flies with two wings: one of them Hope, the other Fear or Awe. The poet, without forgetting to be humble before his Lord, here stresses the idea of hope and offers as his reason for doing so a "theology" reminiscent of a story about Bayazid Bastāmi: Once God spoke to him in a vision and threatened to reveal Bayazid's spiritual infidelity to the world, so that the people might stone him. Bayazid said, "Go ahead.

91

But if You do, I shall reveal to the world the fact that Your Mercy is so much greater than Your justice that no one will ever obey any of Your Laws again!" So they agreed on mutual silence.

'Ayn Al-Qozāt Hamadāni

QUATRAIN

Last night she embraced me
my idol twined her arms round me
caught me and pierced my ear
with the ring of slavery.
I told her, "For your love
I'll roar and shout! and RIOT!! and ..."
but she put her lips to mine
and closed my mouth.

Wahshi Bāfqi

THE PIRATE OF TIME

I would that Love the thief might steal away
existence from my head;
I pray that selflessness might cure
the disgrace of self.
My house is built on bricks of roaring fire:
like a spy I'll open up
the doors and invite some unjust hordes
to plunder my pelf.
I am winter's dried and withered branch

and all the icy cold
of earth can do me no harm: what leaf,
what fruit to freeze?
Stoke up the hell of your injustice:
I am so strong in love
I do not know a flame could move me
from my place.
I pray the Magian vintner's cup may be
declared against the Law
for any reveler who begs
another wine.
O Wahshi, what treasure do you still possess
to steal or not to steal?
Why do you then still quake in fear
of the Pirate of Time?

Everything the lover once possessed is lost in the course of Love. Why should he now fear loss? Only one thing remains to be stolen, and he invites this final annihilation of self. He totters on the verge of extinction, prepared to die into the One.

Sarmad

QUATRAIN

The universe
is a kaleidoscope:
now hopelessness, now hope
now spring, now fall.
Forget its ups and downs:

93

do not vex yourself:
The remedy for pain
is the pain itself.

Sarmad

QUATRAIN

In the Abbatoir of Love they slaughter the good
But make no meat of the thin or of the rude.
You call yourself a lover? Taste the knife!
Those who still live are corpses, not Love's food.

San'at

THE TENTMAKER

She unveils her face
  to the cup: it becomes
  a bright moon;
for those who ask a kiss
  her tongue becomes
  a sword.
My knight, my royal rider
  sits upon the gray horse
  of pride;
I call upon my yearning:
  help me at least to kiss
  the stirrup.
From your garden morning plucks
  a new sunflower to tie
  in her locks;

your dagger-glance cuts sleep
from star-girls' eyes
in night's harem.
For love of the blossom Nightingale
sheds from its eyes tears
of rosewater.
Last night our moral guardian, drunk,
shouldered a wine jug and set out
to the monastery.
San'at, your art is sewing tents for the camp
of the Friend. Weave your ropes from veins
of the soul.

San'at, a poet of the Hindustani style (post-Hāfez, sometimes overly baroque, but at best delicate and original), discusses the attributes or qualities of lover and Beloved. Her Face is reflected in the mirror of the lover's heart, as the sun's light is reflected in the moon, and the lover's Intellect is illuminated. He experiences the attributes of the Beloved: mercy and cruelty, pride and self-sufficiency. But his own capacity is too small to comprehend the mercy or survive the cruelty. He is base, he is in need. The kiss here symbolizes both life and death, or life-in-death: he who makes his heart a home for the Beloved must weave tent ropes with the veins of his own soul: he must die to himself.

Bābā Afzal Kāshāni

QUATRAIN

Thy love makes me alive eternally
Yet Chaos is my life in hunting thee
Till into Spirit thou transform my dust:
What better work? What generosity!

The nature of Love is to plunge the lover in chaos, to "ruin his life," yet at the same time confirm his immortality and, like the Philosopher's Stone, transmute flesh into Spirit.

Sarmad

QUATRAIN

I plucked the rose cups by the garden wall,
Filled sleeves with petals: I desired them all.
The equinox of Spring's overflowing Grace
Is nothing. I desire to bloom in Fall.

"To bloom in Fall": the Resurrection from the dead, rebirth in self-extinction. This state alone insures us against agony and frustration. It is the one and only true enjoyment.

UNION

Like rags and tatters that have tripped him up and hid his true nature, the seeker now sheds the last scraps of his separative existence. Like Majnun, the mad lover, he begins to realize that "I *am* Layla," the girl he has loved so long and lost.

The process of Creation, the "arc of descent," ends with man's total forgetfulness of *who he really is*. The process of Return, the "arc of ascent," is now about to close the circle and reduce all things again to a single point, the Origin itself. All "idols" are to be broken, even the idol of "liberation." Finally, the traveler reaches the level of the Archetypes, the Image Exemplars, and beholds there the Image of the Beloved Herself. But then, something more, the mystery of mysteries: all manifestation, even the highest and purest, is left behind. "Bewilderment" overwhelms the seeker (as the Prophet prayed, "O Lord, increase my bewilderment!") and dissolves the individual awareness in a sea of light. At last he has "arrived," only to find that he had never for even a moment been "away." Not even a tongue remains with which to repeat

There is one and only One:
There is no God but HE.

(Hātef Isfāhāni, *Tarji-band*)

97

Ahmad Ghazāli

SULTAN MAHMUD AND THE SALT VENDOR

Not until TWO has been erased
will lover enjoy Union with Beloved:
one in one is nothing: one a sacrifice
for the other, a banquet for the other.
The lover has a big stomach, true,
but big enough for this treasure? Never!
How can fire be food for the moth?
Withdraw your skirt from such impossibilities.
How can the sun sit in an atom's heart
or the sea be channeled in a drain spout?
The lover's food is his image of the Beloved
not Union itself. One strand of her hair
is too heavy for him—but he himself
is no more than a spoonful for her.
She demands a sacrifice, and his name
is uprooted from the soil of existence:
she can place him like a single strand
of hair amongst her tresses.

> *The lover attains Union only*
> *with being's disintegration,*
> *self's disunion. The very union of his being,*
> *the principle which holds his self together,*
> *is his separation from the Union of Love.*

When the Reality of love appears, the lover
becomes food for the Beloved, where before,
in separation, the lover fed upon his darling.

Just so, the moth, impassioned with the candle's flame, takes nourishment from the fire only at a distance from its glow. Illumination's far march beckons the moth with promises of love, to fly on effort's wings through the air of quiet.

The moth has a means of travel—his powdery wings
but the machine of flight is not the tool
by which he will attain to Union. His round of flight,
the "air of quest," extends no further than the
glowing sphere thrown by the candle into space.
Union with the flame is the station of burning;
flight lasts no further than the fire's borders,
and once the moth surrenders his being to the lamp
he moves no more toward the flame, but feels
the flame now move in him. Fire's love
for the moth now penetrates his being.

A great secret: the moth no longer eats, but is eaten, and for one breath's time becomes his own Beloved. This is perfect consummation, all flight and circumambulation are meant for this instant alone. Ah, but when shall this be? Have we not said that annihilation is the reality of Union? Fire welcomes the lover for one brief hour, then sends him away through gates of ash.

His wings carried him while yet he flew
but Union has burned his wings. Then know
which of the two, the moth or candle,
has Union in its grasp. Know that the

99

instrument for Union lies not with the lover
but with the Beloved.

"In Thy Love
my singleness abounds. "

He whose very existence is pain, a machine
for separation, how can the means of Union
be his? The ground of Union is nonbeing, the
ground of separation is being. While yet you
court the sweetheart of Annihilation, there
remains some hope for Union, but when she
disappears, separation's shadow spreads
itself across the earth and the possibility of
Union is no more; for the lover cannot
possess the means for Union; Union is the
task of the Beloved.

THE TALE:
The zodiac smiled upon a day
when Sultan Mahmud appeared amongst
his courtiers and sat upon his throne.
Suddenly a man burst in with a tray
of salt upon his head and in the midst
of the levée began to cry, "Who will buy?
Who needs my salt?"
                              The Sultan
was dumbfounded by the scandal and at once
ordered the man's arrest. Then, "Leave us alone, "
he commanded, and beckoned the salt man
to approach. "This is a palace, a place

100

where heaven itself prostrates in fear.
Have you imagined it a bazaar, where you might
hawk your wares? How could you be
so rash, so rude? Explain yourself!"
The man replied, "I shall openly reveal
my secret. This salt is but a pretext.
My real intention was to see Ayaz."
Mahmud grew hot with rage. "Beggar!"
he exclaimed. "Do you claim partnership in love
with ME? Would you thrust your hand
into the same dish with the Sultan?
Mine is the realm, the rule, the crown,
the power. Seven hundred elephants at my command,
no king rivals my wealth, my glory—
while you, you have not the bread
for a single night..."

                                "Say no more!"
the man interrupted. "Shall I tell you
the salt's real secret? Are you a lover?
Then arise and prepare yourself for the Path.
This wealth, these elephants, this glory
are but the means of selfishness and pride.
The means for Love is burning pain.

What a tyrant you are! Have you forgotten
the Verses which recount how when Allah
was preparing to place Adam upon the earth,
that host of peacock-feathered angels sang,
'We hymn Thy praise and Sanctify Thee'

(II,30)? And God answered, 'Before you can
praise and sanctify you need to be stripped of
self hood. But if you could do that, you would
no longer be angels, for you have not been
given the power to renounce your selves.'"
The salt vendor continued,

*"If the time for Union arrives, Mahmud,
then Ayaz will possess the means for it,
not you. Angels know not the device of love,
but man, though sinful, is as low as dust;
this lowliness is his privilege,
for it gives him the chance
to die to himself. The stewpot of your love
is empty of salt. Your power and dominion,
your rule in Sind and Hind, what are they worth
without Ayaz?"*

"Nothing . . . ," answered Mahmud.
*"And tell me, without him, is a rose garden
any better than a privy? To be with him
in the dungstore of a public bath, or a ruined house,
is that not better than paradise itself
without him?"*

"You are right," said Mahmud.
*"Then you can never possess the device
for Union, despite your pomp and train.
The beauty of the Beloved is Union's key,
for Union without that beauty is impossible.
The lover's being is but the means of separation*

for he is unworthy to possess Union's device.
If Time's fortune smiles on him he may
succeed in uprooting his very being,
in sacrificing it for that of the Beloved,
and offering up his life and soul to him."
A perfect Love, a beautiful Beloved:
Where in the world could one live such a dream?
The heart would speak and yet the tongue is mute:
I sit athirst beside a flowing stream!

Ahmad Ghazāli was one of the first Persian authors to make use of the symbolism of moth and candle, which later attained the status of a cliché in mystical poetry. The moth first travels as far as the glowing sphere of light around the candle flame and there enjoys its heat and light. This represents the stage of knowledge. But when the moth finally surrenders itself to the fire, it is consumed. This symbolizes a state beyond knowledge, the total Union that can only be attained through the extinction of the lover. No one remains to "know" anything at all.

Ghazāli then expands on nature symbolism with a Sufi interpretation of the love affair between Sultan Mahmud of Ghazni and his beautiful slave boy, Ayaz. The salt vendor chides Mahmud for his selfishness in love. Man, he explains, is a being endowed with will, unlike the blindly instinctual animals, or the angels, who are created without will, and hence without the possibility of either sin or complete perfection in love. In order to attain to this perfection, however, man must pass beyond his own will to knowledge, and even beyond his will to survive as an individual will. All that he "possesses" is merely a cause of his separation from the Divine Beloved. What allows him to realize Union is the realization of his own nothingness and of the complete self-sufficiency of the Beloved.

Ahmad Jāmi

QUATRAIN: THE IDOL

> *As long as one tress-tip*
> > *of the hair of your existence*
> > *still remains*
> *I fear the Sect*
> > *of Self-worship*
> > *will survive.*
> *You claim "I broke*
> > *the Idol of Illusion—*
> > *I'm liberated!"*
> *but I fear*
> > *your Manifesto is itself*
> > *an idol.*

The hair of the Beloved often symbolizes Creation in its *Maya* aspect, manifestation as a veil (or disheveled tresses) over the face of Reality. The greatest sin in Islam

is said to be *sherk*, "association," i.e., associating
something with God in such a way as to make that thing
an "idol," a substitute for God. Exoterically, only the
dualists or polytheists or hypocrites are guilty of *sherk*,
but Ahmad Jāmi here expresses the belief, common to the
Sufis, that even good Muslims, even self-proclaimed
Sufis, practice *sherk-e khafi* or hidden *sherk*. How can they
help but do so, as long as they still think of outward
existence as "real" in itself? Even when they proclaim
themselves "liberated," the very fact that an "I" remains
to make the claim (not to mention the conceit involved in
such a boast) disproves its validity. Ultimately, only the
saints escape from this unconscious "polytheism."

'Ayn al-Qozāt Hamadāni

QUATRAIN: JEALOUSY

"At the shore, at the water's lip,
wash your lips pure . . ."
　　　"But what can I do
　　　with lips that smell of others?"
"Others! With these lips
that have kissed mine
　　　never go lip-to-lip
　　　with someone else!"

Amir Khosraw

THE THRESHOLD

Wasted by desire
            not a trace of me remains:
what can I do? I cannot see
            enough of your face.
All day around your neighborhood
            nights on your threshold
I have no goal but
            a glimpse of you.
I'll have to use my eyes for these
            ritual circumambulations
since I've worn my feet down
            to the knee in my search.
I swear by the loyalty you deserve
            your faithful cur
has fed his heart to the stray dogs
            of your quarter.
Mind, heart, intelligence, eye
            empty of all image
but your face. Unworthy slave, at least
            I offer my soul in your love.
Dead hearts stir to life
            in your cool breeze;
where is the garden that produced
            such expensive perfume?

String two hundred worlds of sorrow like pearls
on my slender body, still
I will not trade a strand of your hair
for this world or the next.
Now no room remains to insert
a word about myself;
in any case the Case of Khosraw
has become a fable
for his search
for you.

In his journey the lover has left behind the separative world of Creation and has reached the threshold of the Beloved. This may be said to symbolize the gnostic's entrance into the Imaginal World, the level of the Archetypes or Image Exemplars. In this interpretation of the poem, Khosraw enjoys the sight of the Beloved, but not yet Union.

San'at

THE LAMP OF YOUR FACE

What need
lovers for world's delights
or the moth
for refined pleasures,
"viewing the garden"?
His lips
parched for water of Union

with the Beloved:
      what need to chase
      the "fountain of Khezr"?
He who falls
      in your quarter, what need
for the caravans
      of paradise except
      to seek your love?
Surrendering his body
      to the couch of your disease
what need has he
      for the "healing breath"
      of Jesus?
If the Friend
      did not sit with him
in his retreat, what need
      for the cloister
      of solitude?
Today he gives up
      his soul to separation:
why should he wait
      for the promise
      of tomorrow?
What need anymore
      for glass after glass
of red wine, intoxicated,
      unconscious with your
      amorousness?

108

I am that moth

at the lamp of your face:

San'at, what do I need

with the candle

of manifestation?

The seeker should direct his attention to nothing but God Himself, as the lover should seek nothing but the Beloved. The Creator, not the creation, is the ultimate object, in keeping with the demands of the "First Pillar" of Islam, Unity *(tawhid)*.

Binavi Badakhshāni

QUATRAIN

I became water

and saw myself

a mirage

became an ocean

saw myself a speck

of foam

gained Awareness

saw that all is but

forgetfulness

woke up

and found myself

asleep.

Ontologically, water and ocean represent Authentic Existence, as opposed to "mirage" or "foam," which stand for the illusory nature of our present phenomenal existence. Epistemologically, Awareness or waking up stands for realization or illumination, a higher state of consciousness, which is contrasted with forgetfulness or sleep, our state of consciousness in the realm of illusion. One set of symbols represents the lower self, the other the higher Self.

Bābā Afzal Kāshāni

QUATRAIN

You must be cross-eyed not to see the Real
Or lack the eyes to look at Him, I feel,
To know that you, from head to toe, are HIM—
The Universal Apple, core and peel.

The oneness of Reality (*wahdat al-wojud*) can only be experienced by one whose inner eye is open. He who is completely "blind" is an unbeliever, a *kafir*. He who sees reality as two is "cross-eyed," an "associationist" (*mushrik*, i.e., one who associates God with other-than-God). *Wahdat al-wojud* is the ontological side of the coin; it describes Being as it *is*. *Wahdat al-shohud*, "Unity of Witness," is the epistemological side of the same coin; it describes Reality as it is *perceived* to be One. He who opens his inner eye and "looks at" the One, thus possesses *wahdat al-shohud*.

Shāh Ne'matollāh

MATHNAWI

I beheld my essence. What I saw
Was like the very light of the eye itself:
How wonderful that a single Essence should
Refract itself like light, a single source
Into a million essences and hues.
The being of the lover and Beloved
Are the same, for where is Love without
A lover and Beloved to be found?
Behold His Essence by His Light, that you
May be yourself the seer and the Seen.
I have wandered through the essences
And found that His Reality makes up
The essence of all beings. To ourselves
We manifest ourselves; were it not so
There could be no relationship between
The One and many. Now then, go beyond
Relation, go beyond the going-beyond
Till there remains no body, soul or being.
"All that is must perish save His face"
And in His Being ours is burned to ash.
At last I see that vision of Him requires
A subject and an object: I and He.
And yet the Essence is the same, sometimes
A wave upon the sea, sometimes the sea;

111

Sometimes the eye, sometimes the object of
The eye. Whoever sees this ocean knows
Our essence as we know it in ourself.
We are the waves and yet in essence we
Are not different from the sea: Reality
Is one but shows itself as two: subject
And object, two in manifestation
But not in Essence: only one Existence
Though countless its attributes. The mystery
Is still too deep for all to understand,
For all to grasp: the supraformal Essence
Is the Beloved and the formal self
The lover——but if you switch the terms around
The statement still remains unchanged and true.
Or if you say the cup and wine are one
That too is true, as true as if you claim
That cup is cup and wine is wine; or if
You say that one is us, the other Him.
Regard these different levels of the truth
As "relatively absolute" and find
The subtle occult truth. Then ... WA SALAAM!
The relativity of intellect
Results in statements which must contradict
Each other on the level of the mind
And yet beyond the mind both are correct.
Sometimes I am Mahmud, sometimes Ayaz
Sometimes I glorify myself, sometimes
I sing the other: lover and Beloved.

So from time to time I change and play
Both roles, and then a third one: Love itself.
Thus spoke Mustafa, beloved of God:
Go, search for the one who has enslaved your heart
Within your heart. There find the satisfaction
Of your soul at last. Seek Ne'matollāh, find
All that you seek—and all that you require
Will then be found in me, as you desire.

This *mathnawi* has been chosen out of a great many similar didactic poems by Shāh Ne'matollāh (and countless other Sufi poets) as an example of the genre. It unpacks again all the metaphorical baggage of the school: the object of sight is said to be identical with the light of the eye (the subject), which perceives it, the single Essence with all individual essences, the lover with the Beloved and with Love itself, the waves with the sea (since they are in reality nothing but water), etc. He ends, however, with a declaration that could only have been made by a Sufi master: that the key to these identities is to be found in him, the "realized" man.

'Ayn al-Qozāt Hamadāni

QUATRAIN

He Who splashed a thousand worlds with color
How can He buy the paint of "I and thou"?
Colors, colors—nothing but whim and fantasy;
HE is colorless, and one must adopt His hue.

Gharib Nawāz

BEWILDERMENT

Tell me: if the hidden treasure is now on display
at the bazaar, shouldn't the gnostic leave his cell
and wander forth?

Tell me: why should he pitch camp on the plain of
manifestation?
No doubt to cast His reflection on the mirror
of Creation ... but

anyway, what do I know? This dream confuses me:
no wonder my liver's upset. Listen,

if creatures were made to reveal Him,
why are they veiled?
But then, of course, veils themselves
are very revealing ...

well then, if I'm His veil I'll make my exit
and let Him become "I," the seer of what is seen.

He'll see Himself in my mirror. He Himself
will become both the seeker and the Sought.

Stop ... ! All I get out of this is a maze of riddles!
Words, words ... If it was difficult before, what a
headache now!

114

If He's the only one who knows Himself,
and we have no share in it,
then tell me: from whom was He hidden
and to whom revealed?

"Only the jeweler who cracks the oyster
can really appreciate the pearl ... and himself **become**
the pearl.

Break the shell of water and clay from heart and soul
that the gloom of your being may be bathed in light.

There is no 'other'——all are mirrors reflecting
the Friend:
you look in the mirror, you see His face——and He
becomes the Beloved.

In the midst of annihilation's feast he who drains
the cup of permanence
will grab the rope of ANA 'L HAQQ and swing
from the gibbet.

If the saki's face reflects in the hermit's glass of red
He'll turn his face to the bar and become a prize drunk

and whoever catches the Beloved's tress
in his little noose
will rip up his rosary and make it a Christian sash. "

115

What is the secret that peeps from behind the curtain
to make these dullards suddenly so ... aware?

I mean: considering God's grace and mercy
it's not surprising if a pious servant should fall into sin.

Ah, when he comes at dawn to visit His patient
all the healthy folk in the neighborhood will play sick.

You are asleep. The Beloved cradles your head
in His lap;
a blessing on your eyes, the day you finally awake!

Who takes one step outside himself—like the leg
of a compass—
will whirl round and round the whole circle ...

So much wine, cup after cup you poured for Mo'in,
his drunken heart has lost the desire to sober up.

The present work might be seen as a commentary
on the famous *hadith* in which God says, "I was a Hidden
Treasure and desired (or loved) to be known, so I created
the world that I might be known." Thus Creation is said
to be a mirror in which God is reflected, and since there
is only One Being, then He who stands before the mirror
must be seeing only Himself. This drama takes place
within man as microcosm: his heart will be the mirror if
and when he drinks the wine of Eternal Being in the

tavern of Annihilation, if he dies to himself. Like Ḥallāj, if he loses his head on the gibbet, he can proclaim, "I am the Truth (or *God*)"—*ana 'l-Ḥaqq*. The poet intensifies the drama by adding to these metaphysical concepts the experience of bewilderment and scandal (symbolized by such images as the drunken hermit and the worshiper who turns his rosary into a Christian sash), for the simultaneous awareness of Unity and multiplicity is quite simply beyond reason, and the fact that the whole of Creation is in a sense a secret that should never have been revealed is a sort of scandal.

Abu Sa'id Abol-Khayr

QUATRAIN

Love came
    flowed like blood
    beneath skin, through veins
emptied me of my self
    filled me
    with the Beloved
till every limb
    every organ was seized
    and occupied
till only
    my name remains.
    the rest is It.

Gharib Nawāz

RIDDLE

Lord,
  whose face is this
    reflected in spirit's mirror?
      Such beauty painted
        on the inner screen—
          who is he?
Each atom
  in all space
    is filled ...
      Who transcends the galaxies,
        shows himself in every molecule—
          who is he?
Sun
  in the costume
    of various specks of dust
      sparks forth various rays
        of light at every moment—
          who is he?
Outwardly
  you appear in the meat
    of our existence
      but he who is hidden
        in soul's marrow
          who is he?
In soul's fête

every now and again he sings
a new song, melodies of peace
touching the veils
of the people of the heart—
who is he?
He who manifests himself
upon himself
makes love to himself
in the name
of lovers
who is he?
How many times, Mo'in
will you drag yourself and me
between us?
He, the goal of I and thou,
is there—right there!
Who is he?

Gharib Nawāz speaks here of Unity in plurality, the
manifestation of the Absolute in the relative: the eye of
the heart, the inner eye, sees God on the screen of the
heart. When it looks at the world "outside," it sees the
same Reality—Truth reflected in everything, in the
smallest creature, the tiniest mote of dust, just as the sun
when it shines casts its light on everything at once.

Lest the reader harbor the least remnant of
dualism—God/world, Absolute/relative—the poet
attempts to deal with every possible sort of

119

misunderstanding that might arise. God has manifested Himself to Himself. He is the Absolute and the relative, lover and Beloved, etc. The Divine "process" is precisely one of Self-manifestation.

In the end, the poet admits that even he has perpetrated a kind of dualism, since by speaking to (or even of) God, he has admitted an "I" and a "thou." He must transcend this, must leap out of himself or over his own shadow and speak from the Station of Divine Awareness itself, where only One exists.

Rumi

A THIEF IN THE NIGHT

Suddenly
  (yet somehow expected)
he arrived
    the guest ...
the heart trembling
    "Who's there?"
    and soul responding
      "The Moon . . ."

came into the house
    and we lunatics
ran into the street
    stared up
    looking

for the moon.

Then—inside the house—
    he cried out
"Here I am!"
    and we
beyond earshot
    running around
        calling him ...
crying for him
    for the drunken nightingale
locked lamenting
    in our garden
while we
    mourning ringdoves
        murmured "Where
where?"

As if at midnight
    the sleepers bolt upright
in their beds
    hearing a thief
break into the house
    in the darkness
they stumble about
    crying "Help!
        A thief! A thief!"
but the burglar himself

    mingles in the confusion
echoing their cries:
   "...a thief!"
     till one cry
       melts with the others.

AND HE IS WITH YOU
   with you
in your search
   when you seek Him
look for Him
   in your looking
closer to you
   than yourself
     to yourself;
Why run outside?
   Melt like snow
wash yourself
   with yourself:
urged by Love
   tongues sprout
from the soul
   like stamens
     from the lily ...

But learn
   this custom
from the flower:

Silence

your tongue.

"And He is with you" (IV, 57). *Tawhid*, Unity in its deepest sense, is the first principle of Religion, which impels the Sufis to claim that all, everything, is He. This is true not merely at that spiritual stage of Intuition in which the seer and Seen are said to be one, but even at the beginning of the Path. For the aspirant himself is said to be the very object of aspiration. Like a thief who mingles unseen with the crowd that pursues him, the object of our search is "closer to us than our jugular vein" (L,16). As Ahmad Ghazāli put it, "We drown in an endless ocean, yet our lips are parched with thirst." As one Sufi poet said,

There's water in the pot yet we wander about
complaining of thirst;
The Beloved's in the house, yet we roam
round the world in our search.

And as Hāfez claims,

For many years the heart sought
Jamshid's Cup from me
Asking from strangers that which
it possessed itself!

JOY

At every stage of the Path there is a "passing-away" and an arrival, a pain and a joy. Joy, thus, is always part of the Path; but he who finally "arrives" is no longer at the mercy of these states, but the master of them. Thus passing-away is not merely a negative experience, not a mere extinction of the seeker into some impersonal pantheistic "beyond." On the contrary, it is now that true existence really begins. The journey from the World to God, and the journey in God, now give way to the journey from God to the World. That World, which once seemed the prison of all awareness, is now seen as a reflection of paradise. Liberation from the world of opposites, of becoming and change, of the limited senses, brings joy and freedom, a sense of floating above the universe on a perpetual holiday/holy day.

Sā'eb Tabrizi

A PERMANENT VACATION

*Our unemployment guarantees a holiday
from even the thought of work
from even a care for profit and loss
in this bazaar.
We take the world so easy that we sleep
the sleep of security
ignoring this wakeful kingdom*

and its bitter war.
We close our eyes and ears and every sense
to every degrading desire and lust;
why should we work to cure all souls
of their foul disease?
Like a rose that lives out the year, our spring
and autumn have merged in one;
the endless flux of the lying world
has set us free.
We make no complaint of the highs and lows of earth
its valleys and hills; its rasp,
like the ridges of a worn-out file,
is smooth at last.

Sa'eb, we'll hide our heads
beneath the wing of life,
flip all the pages of the garden's book.
Have done with strife.

'Erāqi

QUATRAIN

Sing
the matchless pleasure
of gypsy girl
and beggar
    Toss
    cap from head
    fling sandals
    from feet.
So
I kick my life away
and sacrifice
my heart
    Trade
    the caravanserai
    of this world and the next
    for One.

THE PERFECT MAN

The joyful experience of the "dervish," the carefree "cherubinic wanderer," is only a partial reflection of the real Goal and End of the Path: the Perfect Man. He who has finally and totally realized his humanness simultaneously realizes his Godness: "He who knows himself, knows his Lord." It is for the Perfect Man that God created the World, for only he can truly fulfill God's "desire" to be known; and it is for him that God maintains the World in existence. Indeed, if such a man were to say, "I am the Truth," he would simply be stating a fact—since to all intents and purposes, he and God are but one. The "secret" with which we began is now fully uncovered. The Perfect Man, in fact, *is* that secret.

Gharib Nawāz

THE SECOND JESUS

O Lord, it's me: blanked out in divine light
and become a horizon of rays flashing from the Essence.

My every atom yearned for vision
till I fell drunk on the manifestations of lordship.

Love polished the rust from my heart's mirror
till I began to see the mysteries;

127

I emerged from the darkness of existence
and became what I am (you know me) from the
Light of Being:

blackened like charcoal dark soul's smoke
but mixed with love fires and illumined.

Some say the path is difficult;
God forgive them! I went so easily:

The Holy Spirit breathes his every breath into Mo'in—
who knows? Maybe I'm the second Jesus.

Fo'ād Kermāni

LORD OF THE HARAM *

I

Watch out: dawn and revelation
of the eternal face;
Being's King raises battle banners
from the field of Nonexistence.
(Rich man goes to a party:
he needs no servant but
one goes along anyway, gets invited in;
and even that servant

* in Arabic, "sanctuary."

128

is a morning star, gleaning its light
by rubbing its face against Eternity.)

The Unseen, the Forbidden
   when it yearned to reveal itself
and raise its torches high
   above the hidden abyss
to create in its Power
   through the order: "BE!"
before even the Pen
   and Tablet were known
   then 'Ali's heart became the Tablet
   Ahmad's tongue the Pen.

The station of 'Ali, Kaaba's lord, *
   became the Heart itself
and all our circumambulations
   then were abrogated,
all ritual complete——Look!
   The Elect are forbidden
what ordinary men must do
   and outward pilgrimage denied
   to men of Heart, whose pillar is the palace
   of 'Ali, lord of the Haram.

When I turn toward the prayer niche

*Kaaba: building in Mecca toward which Moslems bow in prayer.

129

I journey toward him;
when I begin my prayers
    I speak with him;
        ignoring the road to Mecca.
Passing by the Black House
    I circle his neighborhood:
        to venerate the child born within it
            is all the worship the Kaaba demands.

Mercies are signs
    of the Mercy of 'Ali,
the books of the prophets
        rehearse his tale,
paradise and its fruits
        are his gifts
and the greatest gift of God
        is 'Ali's sacred role.
        *Say yes! for **this***
        is God's greatest favor.

The King: through his tongue
        God addresses man
and with his command will unroll the days
        of Resurrection and Reckoning:
who loves him will have the reward,
        who hates him the fire.
He is beyond all labels
        all names I might bestow:

sovereign of the Arabs
emir of the Persians.

With a smile he bestows being
on the Possibles,
with a whisper he snatches repose
from the breasts of all things,
with kindness and wrath
he gives life and death
but if he withdraws his favor
from all that is other-than-God
with a flick of the finger he'll crush
the theater of the world.

II

Divine Essence is beyond thought.
So cut this philosophic guff:
our minds can never grasp
nor eyes perceive
that absolute Absolute—
so when it comes to **this**
the brain is mired and boggled
in bewilderment
and the foot of perception
stuck in the door.

Even the Universal intellect
cannot comprehend His Essence

131

so how can these paltry flecks
    of gray matter compete?
No one gets to the Essence
    except the Essence.
Only through His Power
    do things attain Permanence.
    How can that-which-does-not-exist
    reach the Absolute?

III

One by one, old and young,
    blind plagiarists cook up
a charming set of "creators"
    out of daydreams;
every one of them low and high
    falls on his face before some idol
but not me! Their ignorance
    will not drown me—
    or else why should I
    have been given an intellect at all?

I will not scrape
    before a god of fantasy,
I will not serve or praise
    what I can comprehend.
But this faith of mine has not made me
    an abstracting puritan:
God manifest in 'Ali's form

is my inner vision's object:
I have not seen the Lord except
in the form of this idol.

IV
That king unveiled and moved
    and we were checkmated;
the essences became the places where
        his attributes were revealed.
Intellectuals are impotent
    in their thoughts of him
for the road of Reason cannot reach
        his pure transcendent Being:
        surely all minds are drowned
        in depths of darkness.

Surely the intellect itself is but
    a tiny drop of his generosity
so how can the intellect grasp
        the fact of his existence?
Here in this station the flight
        of the heart's bird becomes its fall;
no one can know his hiddenness
        for in witnessing him
        bewilderment and amazement come
        with a **rush**! and knowledge evaporates.

133

V

Where is a tongue to tell
the tale of his mouth?
I have reached a point so subtle
my lips are numb;
my heart can find no trace
of his lips' unseen ruby
so I speak the story of his mouth
through his tongue alone
and tell the tale of his own state
in his own speech.

His majesty so supreme
only God can praise him—
how could a panegyrist
eulogize his glory?
The mind cannot open its eye
on the tale of his brightness
so he himself must compose
a paean to himself
for his mystery is hidden
from all but him.

I fling paradise away, for 'Ali
is my heaven:
the lights of its gardens are but
rays from his face;
only the cross-eyed look

for anything else.
The lover of God's Friend is he
who contemplates God's Friend:
the one who hands the keys
of paradise to his lovers.

My life is joyful because
it is a gift from him;
I'll surrender it back with the hope
of giving it in his remembrance.
While I lie in his bonds I rejoice
in delight and sorrow:
O know that all which lovers desire
is his will alone
in pain or festival
enjoyment or retribution.

A doctor prescribes and we assume
the medicine will cure:
the beloved is cruel
for a sign of loyalty.
Expect no faith from a lover
who moans and complains:
the journey of the Sufis is toward
the world of purity,
so equal in their eyes
are health and disease.

VI

'Ali the Approved
           pure soul of Ahmad
soul of the Prophet, sign
           of undying Essence
transcending all fault
           untouched by any flaw:
I swear by our outward religion
           you are the secret of Mohammad
           who called you (in your
           external form) "my cousin."

Whatever is and is not
           you have made and will judge;
you reveal Divine Majesty and Beauty
           you are the locus of revelation
you are the compass point and the moving foot
           emanation and source of emanation
you are the Inner and Outer
           Beginning and End.
           All search begins in you
           and in you ends the pursuit.

The galaxies are Mount Sinai for you,
           you yourself the Fire;
the orient of the world is a horizon
           for your appearance.
How can the heart of Fo'ad pretend

to be ignorant of your presence
when on every side the rays
of your light blaze forth
casting shadows which grow long or short
on all the curtains of the universe?

The image of the Perfect Man, which in general terms is certainly the central concept in Islamic esoterism, crystallizes for some Muslims as a distinct historical individual. For Persian Shi'ite Sufis, particularly since Safavid times, 'Ali ibn Abi Talib (the Prophet's cousin and son-in-law, fourth Caliph, first Shi'ite Imam) has been identified as the Perfect Man. Fo'ād Kermāni's extraordinary poem in praise of 'Ali should be read not in the light of ordinary devotional Shi'ism, but as a product of the "marriage" between esoteric Shi'ism and the Sufism of the school of Ibn 'Arabi. It is extremely popular today with the Iranian Sufi orders.

Since for Sufism in general it is Mohammad himself who is considered the Perfect Man, Fo'ād begins by hinting that Mohammad and 'Ali are of the same "light"; one might say that 'Ali is like a "ray" of the *nur mohammadiyyah* or Prophetic Light. Shi'ites believe that 'Ali was the first convert to Islam; Fo'ād depicts this as a reflection of the Divine "drama" itself, with the Prophet as the "Pen" and 'Ali as the "Tablet," the Universal Intellect and Universal Soul. Or, using the terminology of Ahmad Ghazāli, one might speak of the first appearance of Spirit and Love: the reality of 'Ali would then be Love,

137

Mohammad the Spirit.

'Ali, thus, is seen as the very form of the Divine Beloved on the level of *tashbih* ("similarity," as opposed to *tanzih*, "incomparability"), where it is possible to speak of God as having speech, hearing, and sight, or even eyes, ears, etc. Therefore, says Fo'ād, 'Ali is in fact the actual essence or goal of spiritual striving, which he represents through the symbolism of pilgrimage, outwardly to the Kaaba in Mecca, inwardly to the Perfect Man.

In Part II (these are our own divisions, not the poet's), Fo'ād discusses *tanzih* and asserts that the Absolute in its Absoluteness transcends all knowing, that He in His Heness is beyond all form *(surat)* and can only be (provisionally) spoken of as transformal Reality *(ma 'na)*.

In Part III, Kermāni says that these paradoxes cause some people to worship false idols but that he himself is able to worship God as *both* Immanent *and* Transcendent. However, he is no exoterist, "purifying" God of all attributes or refusing to see Him in the realm of manifestation.

In fact, in a sense 'Ali too has both transcendent and immanent aspects. In Part IV, Kermāni claims that the intellect cannot participate in that aspect of the Perfect Man which is, as it were, turned toward the Absolute. Even when, in Part V, we contemplate the Perfect Man as he turns toward the world, we can find no words with which to describe him. Only he himself can speak accurately of his own state, so the poet must "annihilate" himself in order to be able to hear and record that speech. In the last section, 'Ali is described as God's Friend, the "secret" of Mohammad, the focal point of Creation, the central manifestation (the "Fire" that appears to Moses on Mount Sinai)—in short, the *ensān-e kāmel* or Perfect Man.

Khaqāni

LANGUAGE OF THE BIRDS

I

Morning veiled in woven prisms
breaks the seal of its breath,
    exhales ropes of amber
    for the angels' tents.
        Dawn's flat blade shines
        like a metal page
            with jewels upon jewels.
            Chain mail of the clouds:
                rings linked with rings
                locks within locks.
Cock of the Cosmos
arches wings till the heart
    becomes a bird of joy
    beating pinions on the drum
        of wakefulness: drums

139

of departure sounding
for Sleep's caravan.
A moon raised by sorcery
from a deep well, dawn
climbs from behind the hills
while the real moon herself
lifts slowly from dawn's embrace
like a fish tail splashing,
glimmering above the surface
of a pond.
Sun thrusts his javelin
of alchemic gold and spears
morning's silver ring:
bedouin on a raid
against purple-veiled
nomads of night,
riding, returning again
to the Kaaba in its wandering,
gown of gold streaming
from its shoulders ...
The Kaaba ...
Khaqani!
The Kaaba will be
the patron of your poem!
Ask now the provision stored
for you on Reckoning Day
from the stones around
the well of Zem-Zem.

Men seek the Kaaba's black cube
while children game with dice.
Now you are a man of faith
do not turn your face
from its black face.
Why does it lie so still,
so square upon the earth,
this axis of guidance, unmoving
as the hub of a wheel?
The sky
circumambulates.
The mill wheel
turns on its axle ...
The landlord of this house
is the Lord.
This cube
like a cross-legg'd king,
a dark Arab courted
by fair Romans:
the black house
with its white-shrouded
pilgrims.

II
The treasure, the Lode of Korah,
cannot be found, for it moves
forever beneath the earth.
Now the sun's stirrups

are laden with this hoard-gold,
its saddle jingles with golden flowers
as it rides into the sweet plain
of Aries.
Slow smoke spirals of clouds
revolve within the collyrium wheel
of heaven:
earth's frankincense
woven tight with green threads
into the weft of spring.
Nights grow short like lamps
lit at noon, diminished and faint,
while days grow long
as candles carried through the night
moving swift and proud.
Dregs from Rain's grail
spill upon leaves,
bubbles like crystal balls
of dragonfly magicians
rise to the still fountain's
mirror.
The birds are little boys at their ABCs,
the cleverest a nightingale
reciting his lesson of praise.
Last night the Garden
held a parliament of newborn flowers,
clouds watered the delegates
with liquid silver;

the Garden herself gave them
robes of crimson and saffron
dyed in the vats of Moonlight,
presented by the slaves
of the Morning Breeze.
The conference hall
was lit with rose candles,
Narcissus served sweets
from his yellow tray,
dew drenched the crowd
to shield it
from the Tulip's flames.
Streams cut the meadow
in a chess board where flower-bud pawns
spring from the dust
and branches scatter jewel gifts
to embroider robes sewn
by tailor Lilies
with their needle stamens.
Willow branches fan
wind's perfumed censer ...
Sky, the puppet master,
the stars his dolls ...
A meteor:
spear carrier
of the Night.

III

At such an assembly—
when Night was grown thin
and black as a fiddle string
with a crescent moon for a bow—
the birds gathered
to debate their love.
The Ringdove first
praises the Bee, whose saliva
makes bitter petals sweet.
The Nightingale exalts his Rose
who rides as in a royal coach,
the flowering branches
her trailing grooms.
The Turtle sings the nation
of the Cypress, whose smallest breath
can shatter the dome of blooms;
but Starling calls the Cypress "lame,
one-legg'd, sunk in earth—
while Tulip, in blood-red revolt,
conquers field after field."
Wood pigeon says "Tulip by nature
is two-colored, false. The Lily now,
the Lily all white like the
Book of the Righteous..."
But Quail hymns the green Lawn,
"for how can the Garden
write its Book except upon

144

that emerald page?"
Parrot loves Jasmine
more than any vulgar grass,
Jasmine's amber breath
and camphor face;
but Hoopoe longs
for Narcissus, her kingdom
the footstool of Jamshid,
the throne of Afrasiyab.

IV
Strife grew bitter,
birds could reach no end,
so took their pleas
to Simorgh, king of all,
judge of wing'd ones,
master of the necks
of his subjects.
The guardians of the Curtain
saw them approach and warned
"This is the Sanctuary of Grandeur
and the entrance
is very
narrow!"
Ringdove answered
"The flames of my sighs
have burned the Sky's green pavilion.
Show me in or I shall crisp

145

> your curtain to
> cinders!"
> The birds stood milling at the gate,
> Simorgh cloistered within,
>> while Ringdove argued with the guards.
>> At last a messenger of the Unseen
>>> reported all this to the King
>>> who suddenly appeared, called them in
>>> and asked them to speak.
> Nightingale fell in awe
> before the King, bidding him "Good day!"
>> then answering himself, "Good day!"
>> But Turtledove spoke eloquently:
>>> "O thou by whose justice a stolen fig
>>> sticks in the Crow's throat,
>>>> O thou whose fires have forged
>>>> the beak of Partridge like a pair of scissors
>>>>> and painted patterns on the wings
>>>>> of eagles,
> We have brought you our headaches
> (even though spring's chariot
>> drawn by its dappled pair
>> has come sprinkling rosewater
>>> on Earth's troubled brow
>>> giving back intelligence and youth
>>>> to idiot Time):
> Of the infinite army of flowers
> with which shall we rejoice?

Of all these beauties
which think you worthy
to be sovereign
of our love?"

V

Simorgh raised his head and spoke:
"In all this tribe——the hands of one
blushing with henna,
tresses of another
dyed with saffron, indigo——
each of these newborn buds
the child of a dark-eyed houri
now sipping milk
from the creeks of Paradise,
now wine——
each fascinates the heart.
But most exquisite of them all
is that Mohammadan Rose
whose seed is the sweat of Mustafa
while the rest are of water and clay:
that Guide who served the folk he led.
Unlettered One whose words were Truth,
Emperor of the Eighth Paradise,
Master of the Fourth Book.
From every worldly king
he receives tribute,
bestows crowns on all prophets.

At his threshold Intellect
    found the word of forgiveness
    for its pride
Ahmad,
'he who is sent'
    with sparks from his sword
    burned up the thrones of kings
      and roasted the flesh
      of lions.
Prophets
crouch at his gate,
    waiting for handouts
    from the merchant whose charity
      sustains them.
He was, before Adam lay
between water and clay,
    and Adam's son was Jesus:
    how noble Muhammad
      whose fathers
      were his own children!
Earth becomes
a lizard's skin,
    the wheel of heaven
    a green hide to cover
      the hilt and scabbard
      of his sword;
the sun
threads motes of dust

148

from his doorstep in two hundred whips
to enforce the Holy Law
on the world of angels;
the morning star
in shivering fear
breaks the strings of her lute,
untunes the music
of the spheres.
Have you not seen
in days of war that full moon
leading his armies up and along
steep and winding
mountain paths?
For the Leopards of Faith
he transmutes oceans
into dry mirage;
for fiery sea monsters
who protect our religion
he makes the mirage
again an ocean.
Leopards spring
and the lions of predestination
lie helpless in their claws;
the fish of heaven who turns the year
breaks its fangs in fear
of those holy monsters.
To the Prophet's aid
ranks of angels run

swift as lions of the veldt
drawing the scimitars
of the Unseen.
Beneath his flag
'Ali, Commander of the Honeybees,
waves like a date palm
his leaf-tip dart
till his enemies drown
in a whirlpool of blood
deep as a hundred spheres:
that dart, the **aleph**
of a single needle,
unsews the tangled threads
of unbelief.
Gabriel descends again,
reveals the Day of Victory!
O angels, hurry to the war.
O djinn and men
attack!"

VI

Khaqani's poetic taste
Is only for the praise of Mustafa
in view of all the infinite reward
He now expects on Resurrection Day.

How could his subtlety degrade
The value of the coin of precious words

On other than the Prophet? How could a jeweler fling
His pearls into a mirey swamp? What waste!

Then God release me from this jail,
This prison in Shirwan, city of swine,
Citadel of bestial hatreds. Save
Me from this shame, and from Death's Way.

Thou knowest he has no other hope
Who calls on Thee,
    Forsaken by the world, to set him free:
Thy Khaqani.

Khaqāni, one of the most elegant and worldly of all
Persian poets, was criticized by some Sufis for daring to
write on such a mystical subject as the language of the
birds (*manteq al-tayr*, the same title used by 'Attār, Ahmad
Ghazāli, and other Sufi writers). But strong cosmological,
philosophical, and mystical themes underlie this polished,
obscure, and seemingly purely poetic work. Khaqāni's
garden can be seen as the world in miniature, each of his
birds an individual soul loving an individual
manifestation of the Divine Beauty, or "worshiping his
own particular Lord," as Ibn 'Arabi would put it.
Confused as man must be in this world of multiplicity
without the vision of Unity, they take their quarrels to the
Simorgh; they penetrate the veil, take heaven by storm,
in their desire for Truth. The Rose, Mohammad, the
Mohammadan Light (which already existed "while

Adam was between water and clay," so that all the myriad prophets are in a sense but the children of Mohammad), the first Creature, the first Intellect, the noblest of all beings: only this flower, according to the Simorgh, is worthy of love and praise. The beloved of God alone deserves to be the beloved of all. Wild metaphors, botanical trivia, theological curiosities, abstruse speculations on astrology and mythology, paradox, hyperbole—Khaqāni orchestrates his material into a panegyric on the Perfect Man, the Rose at the center of Paradise, of Reality itself.

SOURCES OF THE POEMS

LEAVING THIS WORLD BEHIND

P. 21   Sarmad. "Quatrain: Life's Illusion." *Robā'iyyāt-e Sarmad*, Persian text with Urdu translation, ed. and trans. Sayyed Nawwab 'Ali Sawlat (Delhi, n.d.), p. 87.

P. 22   Najmoddin Kobrā. "Quatrain." Rezd Qoli Hedāyat, *Riyaz al-'ārefin*, ed. Mehr 'Ali Gorgāni (Tehran, 1344 S.*), p. 231. (Also attributed to 'Umar Khayyām.)

P. 23   'Attar. "The Human Case." Faridoddin 'Attar, *Diwān*, ed. S. Nafisi (Tehran, 1339 S.), pp. 29-32.

P. 27   Sarmad. "Quatrain: The Death Trap." *Robā'iyyāt-e Sarmad*, p. 21.

P. 27   Sanā'i. "Stale Loaves." Majdud ibn Adam Sanā'i, *Diwān*, ed. M. Razawi (Tehran, 1354 S.), p. 592.

P. 32   Bābā Afzal Kāshāni. "Quatrain." Afzaloddin Kāshāni, *Musannafāt, vol. 11*, ed. M. Minavi and J. Mahdavi (Tehran, 1337 S.), pp.13-747.

THE SECRET: THE FIRST MEETING

P. 36   Abu Sa'id Abo'l-Khayr. "Quatrain." Mohammad ibn al-Monawar, *Asrār al-tawhid fi maghāmāt al-Shaykh Abu Sa 'id* (Tehran, 1348 S.), p. 340.

P. 37   Shamsoddin Maghrebi. "The Game." Mohammad Shirin (Shamsoddin) Maghrebi, *Diwān* (Tehran, 1348S.), pp.91-92.

F. 38   'Ayn al-Qozāt Hamadādāni. "Fragment." 'Ayn al-Qozāt Hamadāni, *Nāmehā-ye 'Ayn al-Qozāt*, vol. 1, ed. A. Osseyran and Monzavi (Tehran, 1969), p. 282.

P. 39   Shāh Jahāngir Hāshemi. "The Tale of the Uniquely Beautiful Mirror Maker." Shāh Jahāngir Hāshemi, *Mazhar al-āthār*, ed. S. H. Rashidi (Karachi, 1957), p. 63.

P. 42   Salmān Sāvāji. "The Drunken Universe." *Ganj-i-soxan*, vol. II, ed. Z. Safa (Tehran, 1976), pp. 296-97.

*When given according to Islamic dating, years are marked S. standing for A.H.S. (Anno hegira solaris).

153

P. 45   Mahmud Shabestari. "The Spilled Cup." Mahmud Shabestari, *Golshan-e-rāz*, in Mahmud Lahiji, *Maftitih al-e 'jāz fi sharh-e Golshan-e rāz* (Tehran, 1337 S.), p. 762.

AWAKENING

P. 47   Nezāmi. "The Insightful Indian Sage." Abu Mohammad Elyas Nezāmi, *Makhzan al-asār*, ed. W. Dastgerdi (Tehran, 1343 S.), pp. 130-31.

P. 50   'Ayn al-Qozā Hamadāni. "Fragment." *Nāmehā-ye 'Ayn al Qozāt*, p. 282.

P. 51   Sanāi. "Invocation." Hakim Majdud ibn Adam Sanā'i, *Sanāi abād*, in *Mathnawiha-ye Sanāi*, ed. M. T. Razawi (Tehran,1348 S.), pp. 71-72.

P. 52   Sanā'i. "Meditation." Ibid., p. 71.

P. 54   Shāh Dā'i Shirāzi. "Exhortation to an Expedition to the Interior." Shāh Dā'i Shirāzi, *Kolliyyat*, part II, ed. M. Dabirsiyaqi (Tehran, 1339 S./1960), pp. 264-67.

P. 59   Hāfez. "The Vagabond Heart." Shamsoddin Mohammad Hāfez, *Diwān*, ed. M. Qazwini and Q. Ghani (Tehran, n.d.), p. 151.

P. 61   'Ayn al-Qozāt Hamadāni. "Quatrain." *Nāmehā-ye 'Ayn al-Qozāt*, p. 216.

TRANSCENDENCE AND PARADOX

P. 62   'Attār. "Impossible" *Diwān*, p. 545.

P. 64   'Ayn al-Qozāt Hamadāni. "Fragment." *Nāmehā-ye 'Ayn at Qozāt*, p. 197.

SEPARATION AND SADNESS

P. 65   Hāfez. "Letter to the Shaykh of Jām" *Diwān, pp.* 6-7 (with a variant reading of line 5 from *Ghazalhā-ye Hāfez*, ed. Khanlari [Tehran, 1977], p. 5).

P. 67   'Ayn al-Qozāt Hamadāni. "Quatrain: Forbidden Harem." *Nāmehā-ye 'Ayn al-Qozāt, p.* 282.

P. 68   'Ayn al-Qozāt Hamadāni. "Quatrain: A Door Knocker." Ibid., p. 284.

P. 126   'Erāqi. "Quatrain." Fakhroddin 'Erāqi, *Kolliyyāt* (Tehran, n.d.), p. 305.

THE PERFECT MAN

P. 127   Gharib Nawāz. "The Second Jesus." Mo'inoddin Chishti, *Diwān*, p. 140.

P. 128   Fo'ād Kermāni. "Lord of the Haram." Fatollah Qodsi (Fo'ād Kermāni), *Sham'e jam* (Tehran, 1351 S.), pp. 61-63.

P.139   Khaqāni. "Language of the Birds." Khaqāni Shervāni, *Gozidah-e 'ash'ār-e Khaqāni Shervāni*, ed. Z. Sajjadi (Tehran, 1315 S.), pp. 16-22.

BIO-BIBLIOGRAPHIES

Besides the translations listed in the bio-bibliographies, the interested reader may want to consult some general works. By far the best is E. B. Browne's *Literary History of Persia* (London, 1928) in four volumes. Most of our poets are mentioned in it, and in many cases full biographies are given. Browne offers at least one translation of nearly every author he mentions, and the translations are generally of very high quality. Moreover, the book is entertaining; Browne never misses a chance to tell an amusing anecdote. A. J. Arberry's *Classical Persian Literature* (London, 1967) is not so encyclopedic a work, but is very informative on the authors he covers. J. Rypka's *History of Persian Literature* (Dordrecht, 1968) is in some ways more up-to-date than either of these works, despite the author's Marxist attitudes.

ABU SA'ID ABO'L-KHAYR

Shaykh Abu Sa'id Abo'l-Khayr of Mayhana (born 357/967–68, died 440/1049) was a Sufi master famous for his expansive and joyful mysticism and for his sense of humor. He lived in Nishapur. He is said to have been the first Sufi to write rubā'iyyat, but this is now widely disputed. The most authentic source for his life was written long after his death by his great-great-grandson; this marvelous biography, Asrār al-tawhid (*The Secrets of God's Mystical Oneness*, [Costa Mesa, 1992]), has been published in an English translation by J. O'Kane in the Persian Heritage Series. An excellent source is the essay in R. A. Nicholson's *Studies in Islamic Mysticism* (Cambridge, England, 1921).

AHMAD GHAZALI

Ahmad Ghazāli was the younger brother of the famous philosopher-theologian Abu Hamed Ghazāli (known to the medieval West as Algazel). Ahmad was born about 453/1061 in Tus, near Mashhad; he studied there and in Nishapur, was initiated into Sufism at an early age, and became a Sufi master. He traveled around Persia

158

(as far as Baghdad) as a preacher, acquiring numerous disciples, the most famous being 'Ayn al-Qozāt Hamadāni (q.v.). He wrote a number of tracts in Persian and Arabic (of which one, on the "spiritual concert" or samā, has been translated by J. Robson in *Tracts on Listening to Music* [London, 1938]). His most famous work, the first Persian treatise on the metaphysics of Love, called the *Sawāneh*, has been imitated many times. It was put into verse about two hundred years after Ghazāli's death (520/1126 in Qazvin) by the well-known Sufi Mahmud ibn 'Ali Kāshāni (author of the *Mesbah al-hedāyat*, a Persian version of Shahaboddin 'Umar Sohrawardi's *Awaref al-ma'aref*, translated into English by H. Wilberforce Clarke in 1891 [*A Dervish Textbook*, New York, 1970]). Kāshāni's version of the *Sawāneh*, called the *Konuz al-asrār*, has also been attributed to Sanā'i (q.v.) under the title *'Ishq-nāma*. Our selection is based on both the original prose and the later poetic versions. A complete English translation, with commentary, of *Sawāneh: Inspirations from the World of Pure Spirits* by N. Pourjavady has been published [London, 1986]; the translator is preparing a revised version of this work to appear in the latter months of 2000.

AHMAD JAMI

Ahmad Jāmi or Ahmad-e Jām, born 440/1048 in Namaq, settled in Jām (near the present-day Afghan border). After a dissolute youth, he underwent a conversion experience and became famous for his austerity and love of seclusion; he spent eighteen years alone in the mountains near Jām studying the Koran and religious sciences. At age forty he began to initiate disciples, write books, and travel around Khorasan. He made the Pilgrimage to Mecca late in life, and died on his return in 536/1141. He was buried in his *khaneqah* in Jām, which is today a center of pilgrimage and of a special kind of Sufi folk music supposed to have originated with him or been cultivated by him.

AMIR KHOSRAW

Yaminoddin Abu'l-Hasan Amir Khosraw Dehlavi, born 651/1253 in Patyali of a Turkish family, was a courtier and disciple of the great Chishti shaykh, Nizamoddin Awlia (died 724/1324). He wrote in

Persian, and is said to have been one of the first poets to use Urdu. He composed a *khamsa*, or "quintet," in imitation of Nezāmi (q.v.), numerous lyrics and narrative poems, and a prose account of Nizamoddin's life and sayings. Hāfez (q.v.) admired him. He died in Delhi in 725/1325 and was buried next to his master. A biography written by Muhammad Habib was published in 1927 (*The Life and Works of Hazrat Amir Khusrau of Delhi,* [Aligarh,1927]).

'ATTAR

Faridoddin 'Attār, the pharmacist of Nishapur, was a spiritual descendent of Najmoddin Kobrā (q.v.). His dates are very uncertain; the year of his death varies from source to source by as much as forty years, but he probably died around 628/1230 (which would make it impossible for him to have met Rumi's [q.v.] family fleeing from Balkh, or for him to have been killed in battle during the Mongol attack on Nishapur). He is said to have written as many books as there are chapters in the Koran. His most famous are *Manteq at-tayr (The Conference of the Birds,* translated into prose by C. S. Nott [London, 1974], and translated into poetry by Dick Davis and Afkham Darbandi [London, 1984]); the *Ilāhi-nama* (translated by J. A. Boyle [Manchester, 1978]); the *Tazkirat al-awlia (Moslem Saints and Mystics,* translated by A. J. Arberry [London, 1973]); and a *diwān,* of which, unfortunately, very little has been translated.

'AYN AL-QOZAT HAMADANI

'Abdollāh ibn Mohammad 'Ayn al-Qozāt Hamadāni, the great philosopher and mystic, was born in Hamadan in 492/1098, and executed thirty-three years later in Baghdad on a charge of heresy. He studied the works of the famous Abu Hamed Ghazāli and became a disciple of his brother Ahmad (q.v.), with whom he carried on an interesting correspondence. His most important work is the *Tamhidāt* (available in a French translation by Christiane Tortel, *Les Tentations metaphysiques,* [Paris, 1992]), but the only book by him to have been translated into English is his apologia, the *Shakwa'l-gharib,* written in jail shortly before his death. (See *A Sufi Martyr,* by A. J. Arberry [London,1969]; also, *Truth and Narrative: The Untimely Thoughts of Ayn al-Qozāt* by Hamid Dabashi [Surrey, 1999]).

BABA AFZAL KASHANI

Bābā Afzaloddin Mohammad Kāshāni, the eminent philosopher and Sufi, was a contemporary of Nasiroddin Tusi and died in his own native village of Mara outside Kashan about 610/1213. Despite the fact that he composed important treatises in Persian on Peripatetic philosophy, his legendary image is that of an ecstatic lover, and his mystical quatrains are very popular.

BINAVI BADAKHSHANI

Little is known of him other than what Hedāyat says of him in *Riaz al-'ārefin*: that he was a Sufi, initiated by his own father. Presumably, he was from Badakhshan, a remote region of what is now Afghanistan.

'ERAQI

Fakhroddin Ibrāhim 'Erāqi was born in Hamadan but at an early age followed a group of wandering dervishes to Multan (in what is now Pakistan), where he received initiation from Shaykh Baha'oddin Zakariyya Sohrawardi, whose successor he became. In Qonya he studied the *Fusus al-hikam* of Ibn 'Arabi (q.v.) under the great Sadroddin Qonyawi, and there composed his masterpiece, the *Lama'āt* (*Divine Flashes* [Ramsey, 1982], translation by W. C. Chittick and P. L. Wilson). He died in 688/1289 in Damascus and was buried near Ibn'Arabi, whose thought he had helped introduce to the Persian-speaking world. (See also A. J. Arberry's translation of his *'Ushshaq-nama* as *The Song of Lovers* [London, 1939].)

FO'AD KERMANI

Fatollah Qodsi Kermāni (born 1270/1853-54, died 1340/1921-22) was a dervish of the Ne'matollāhi order. His *diwān*, made up entirely of gnostic and Shi'ite poetry, is much admired by Sufis today.

FORUGHI

161

Abbas Forughi Bastāmi, born 1213/1798 in Iraq, came to Bastam in Māzandaran (the birthplace of the famous third/ninth-century Sufi,Bayazid Bastami) after his father's death. He was not a Sufi master, but was probably a dervish, and his mystical love poetry is highly esteemed in Iran today. He was patronized by Nasiroddin Shāh Qājār. He died in 1274/1857.

GHARIB NAWAZ

Khwaja Mo'inoddin Chishti Sanjari Ajmeri, called Gharib Nawāz,was born in Sistan (dates of his birth and death are not certain) and was eighth in succession as head of the Chishti order. He traveled widely around Iran and met most of his major contemporaries in Sufism. Late in his life, he ventured to India where he achieved such enormous success that, although the Chishti order is today forgotten in Persia, it is the most widespread Sufi brotherhood in the Subcontinent. He died and was buried in Ajmer (circa 633/1236), and his exquisite shrine there is called "the Mecca of India." The *diwān* attributed to him, we are informed by friends in India, is probably not authentic; but the poems are obviously written by someone of an exalted spiritual station, which seems to us reason enough to read them. For a hagiographic view of his life, see *The Holy Biography of Hazrat Khwaja Muinuddin Chishti of Ajmer* by W. D. Begg (Ajmer, India). A more scholarly approach will be found in P. M. Curry, *The Shrine and Cult of Muin Al-Din Chisti of Ajmer*, published in India by Oxford University Press. For information on the Chishti literary tradition, see *Notes From a Distant Flute* by Bruce B. Lawrence (Tehran, 1979), and *Burnt Hearts: The Chisti Sufi Order in South Asia and Beyond* (Surrey, 1999) by Bruce Lawrence and Carl Ernst.

HAFEZ

Shamsoddin Mohammad Hāfez was without doubt the greatest lyricist of Persian literature. There are scholars who, misunderstanding his praise of wine, women, and song, have denied that he was a Sufi; one wonders if they can have really read the poems with an open mind. Certainly the Sufis themselves have never doubted he was one of them; they chant his poems in their meetings even today.

"Hāfez" means one who has memorized the entire Koran. A busy life as a religious scholar and courtier prevented Hāfez from compiling his poems into a *diwān*, or from accepting any of the many invitations to attend courts as far away from his beloved Shiraz as India. He died in 791/1389, and his garden shrine in Shiraz is a popular pilgrimage. For the best translations of his poems see Wilberforce Clarke's very literal versions (London, 1974), Gertrude Bell's poetic versions (London, 1928), and the free-verse renditions of J. Heath-Stubbs and Peter Avery (London, 1952). Elizabeth Gray has recently produced a nice edition with translations of fifty ghazals, *The Green Sea of Heaven* (Ashland, 1994).

HATEF ISFAHANI

Sayyed Ahmad Hātef Isfahāni, a relatively minor Sufi poet of the twelfth/eighteenth century, is famous for his one long *tarji-band* on the subject of the Unity of Being. E. G. Browne has translated it quite well in his *Literary History of Persia* (London, 1928), vol. IV, pp. 284-97.

HELALI

Nuroddin (or Badroddin) Helāli Estarābādi, born and raised in Estarabad toward the end of the ninth/fifteenth century, later moved to Herat. There, in 939/1532-33, he was executed by the ruler 'Obayd Khan Uzbek on a charge of Shi'ism and for having circulated a poem insulting 'Obayd Khan. He wrote three famous *mathnawis: Sefat al-'āsheq'in, Layla wa Majnun*, and *Shāh wa dervish* (translated into German by H. Ethé [Leipzig, 1870]).

KHAQANI

Afzaloddin Ibrāhim 'Ali Sherwāni was born in 500/1106–7 in Ganja or Sherwan (both in the former U.S.S.R.). He was a "poet's poet," obscure and difficult, deeply involved in literary and political quarrels (he spent some time in jail), and famous for his wit and elegance. He wrote poems, usually *qasidahs* (odes), on a wide range of subjects. He died in 582/1185 in Tabriz. Although there is no evidence of his having been a Sufi, he was undoubtedly—despite his worldliness—a religious man and deeply influenced by esoteric ideas.

MAGHREBI

Shamsoddin Mohammad Shirin Maghrebi was about sixty when he died in 809/1406–7 in Tabriz. His name ("The Westerner") is said to reflect the fact that he traveled in North Africa, where he was initiated by a shaykh of the line founded by Ibn 'Arabi (q.v.). Leonard Lewisohn has published a critical edition of Maghrebi's *Diwan* (London, 1993).

MAHMUD SHABESTARI

Born around the middle of the seventh/thirteenth century near Tabriz, Shabestari died about 720/1320. Aside from a few treatises, he wrote only the long poem *Golshan-e rāz*, which is considered a major masterpiece of Persian Sufism. The whole poem was composed in the month of Shawwal in 710 (February–March 1311) in reply to fifteen questions sent to Shabestari by a Sufi in Herat named Amir Hosayni. Of the several inadequate translations, the best is probably Whinfield's (first edition, London, 1880), but it is to be hoped that someone someday will undertake a new translation based on, and including at least part of, the important commentary by Abdol Razzaq Lahiji (see "Sources of the Poems," p. 162). A study of his work by Leonard Lewisohn has been published under the title *Beyond Faith and Infidelity* (Surrey, 1995).

MOHYIDDIN IBN 'ARABI

Abu Bakr Mohammad ibn al-'Arabi al-Hatemi al-Ta'i is the one non-Persian who must be mentioned in this anthology because of his profound influence on Persian Sufi thought and poetry. He was born in Murcia in southern Spain in 560/1165. He was educated in Seville, where he was deeply influenced by two women Sufis. He traveled in Spain and North Africa, then in Egypt, Arabia, and Syria, meeting many Sufis. The tale of his wanderings and visions is long; he himself wrote voluminously about them, and in fact is said to have composed seven hundred or eight hundred works in all, some of them comprising many volumes. His philosophy of the Unity of Being, which we have tried to explain to some extent elsewhere in this book, was destined to attract even more followers in the Eastern lands of Islam than in the West. He died in Damascus in 638/1240, "leaving," as S. H. Nasr puts it, "an indelible mark upon the whole spiritual life of Islam." See R. Austin's *The Bezels of Wisdom* (Ramsey, 1980), a translation of the Fusus al-hikam, or his *Sufis of Andalusia* (London, 1971), a translation of the *Risalat al-quds*; and R. A. Nicholson's *The Interpreter of Desires* (London,1978), a translation of the *Tarjuman al-ashwaq*, a collection of Ibn 'Arabi's Sufi love poems. Other studies of Ibn 'Arabi are: T. Izutsu, *Sufism and Taoism* (Tehran, 1979); H. Corbin, *Alone With the Alone: Creative Imagination in the Sufism of Ibn 'Arabi* (Princeton, 1969); and *Quest for the Red Sulphur: The Life of Ibn 'Arabi* (Cambridge, 1993) by Claude Addas. Among William Chittick's works on Ibn 'Arabi are *The Sufi Path of Knowledge* (Albany, 1989) and *The Self-Disclosure of God* (Albany, 1998). See also the French scholar Michel Chodkiewicz, *Seal of the Saints* (Cambridge, 1993) and *An Ocean Without Shore* (Albany, 1993).

NAJMODDIN KOBRA

Born 540/1145 in Khiva in the area known as Khwarazm, Najmoddin Kobrā lived there much of his life. He studied in Nishapur and also in Egypt, in Alexandria, where he became a disciple of Abu Najib Sohrawardi's disciple Ruzbehan al-Wazzan al-Mesri. Najmoddin himself became a great Sufi shaykh and founded the Kobrawi order. He died in 618/1221, killed in battle by the invading Mongols.

NASIMI

Nasimi was born in Baghdad and wrote in Persian and Turkish. Gibb, in his *History of Ottoman Poetry*, calls him "the first true poet of the Western Turks." Nasimi was an initiate of the Hurufi sect (see the article in the *Encyclopedia of Islam*), which was considered heretical. He was executed—skinned alive—in Aleppo in 820/1417–18. See Kathleen Burrell, *The Quatrains of Nesimi, Fourteenth Century Turkic Hurufi* (The Hague, 1972).

NEZAMI

Abu Mohammad Elyās Nezāmi was born in Ganja in 535/1140–41.
Although he followed the custom of dedicating his works to various
princes and rulers, he is said to have spent most of his life quietly at
home tending his family and garden, and was famous for his quietistic
piety. Modern scholars tend to ignore Nezāmi's own professions of
mysticism, preferring to see him as a worldly and elegant poet, but
there is no doubt that he was initiated into Sufism (by Shaykh Akhu
Faraj Zanjani). His life work was the *Khamsa* or "Quintet," five long
narrative poems: *Makhzan al-asrār*, *Khosraw wa Shirin*, *Layla wa Majnun*,
Eskandar-nāma, and *Haft paykar*. The Alexander romance was translated
by Wilberforce Clarke (London, 1881). *Layla and Majnun* (New
Lebanon, 1997) and the *Haft paykar* (London, 1976) are available in
prose translations by E. and G. Hill from the German versions by R.
Gelpke. See also P.Chelkowski's *Mirror of the Invisible World* (New
York, 1975).

RABI'AH BENT KA'B

Rābi'ah, who lived in the fourth/tenth century, was the first poetess of
Persian literature. Her father, Ka'b, may have been the ruler of Balkh
(in what is now Afghanistan). She is said to have been killed by her
own brother because of her love affair with one of his slaves. There is
no evidence of her having been a Sufi, but her love poems have always
been admired by the Sufis. (Do not confuse with the early Sufi saint
Rābi'ah al-Adawiyya [see chapter three] whose words have been
translated by Charles Upton, *Doorkeeper of the Heart*, [Putney, 1988]).

RUMI

Mawlana Jalāloddin Rumi was born in Balkh (in what is now
Afghanistan) in 604/1273. He is undoubtedly the best-loved and best-
known Persian Sufi poet. For his life and works, see A. Schimmel, *The
Triumphal Sun* (London, 1978). For a study of his thought, see W. C.
Chittick, *The Sufi Path of Love*, Albany, 1983). Translations of his works
include R. A. Nicholson's *Rumi, Poet and Mystic* (London, 1973); *Selected*

Poems from the Divani Shamsi Tabriz (Cambridge, 1977); *The Mathnawi of Jalâlu'ddin Rumi* (three-volume edition, London, 1977); A. J. Arberry's *Discourses of Rumi* (New York, 1972), *Mystical Poems of Rumi* (Chicago, 1968), and *The Rubâiyat of Jalâl al-Din Rumi* (London, 1949). See also *Legends of the Sufis*, selections from the *Manaqibu'l 'Arifin by Shemsu'ddin Ahmed, el Eflaki*, translated by J. W. Redhouse (London, 1977); and *Rending the Veil*, translations by Shahram Shiva (Prescott, 1995).

SA'EB TABRIZI

Mirza Mohammad 'Ali Sâ'eb Tabrizi was born in Abbasabad near Isfahan (his father was from Tabriz) and died in 1080/1669–70 in Isfahan. Some consider him the last great Persian poet. He visited India, where he was lavishly patronized and where his work is still extremely popular. He returned to Persia when news reached him that his father was dying, and he later became court poet under Shah Abbas II.

SALMAN SAVAJI

Jamâloddin Salmân Savâji was born about 700/1300 and died in 778/1376. By extemporizing verses in praise of the Il-Khanid ruler Shaykh Hasan Bozorg in Baghdad, Sâvâji became a court poet. He was highly favored by the next ruler, Hasan's son Uways. Sâvâji's poetry was greatly admired and even imitated by Hâfez (q.v.).

SANA'I

Hakim Abo'l-Majid Majdud ibn Âdam Sanâ'i was born in Ghazna and died around 545/1150. One of Iran's greatest poets, and certainly the first great Sufi poet, he was the first to compose long *mathnawis* on Sufi themes (for example the *Hadiqat al-haqiqat*, the first book of which is translated as *The Enclosed Garden of the Truth* by J. Stephenson [New York, 1972]). Other well-known works include a *miraj-nâma*, the *Sayr al-'ebad*, and a *diwân*, both of which merit translation. See also J. T. P. De Bruijn, *Of Piety and Poetry: The Interaction of Religion and Literature in the Life and Works of Hakim Sanâ'i of Ghazna* (Leiden, 1983).

SAN'AT

Mohammad 'Āref San'at was born around 1215/1800 in India in the town of Shikarpur, of a Punjabi family. He worked as a schoolteacher but later took up the family trade of tailoring and tent-making. He was a popular and outgoing person, but ended his life (in 1266/1849) in seclusion in protest against British oppression. Besides his *diwan*, he also composed a *mathnawi* on the famous story of the conversation between Jesus and the skull of the sultan of Baghdad.

SARMAD

Sarmad was said to have been a Jewish merchant of Sabzewar in Iran who, like 'Erāqi (q.v.), fell in love with a dervish boy and followed him to India. Having converted to Islam, he became a "naked fakir"and scandalized the exoteric authorities of Delhi. He was executed by the Emperor Aurengzeb in 1070/1659–60. According to a gentleman we met at Sarmad's tomb outside the Friday Mosque in Old Delhi (an unlikely place to bury a heretic?), Sarmad's last words were:

Beautiful beloved or black executioner:
in whatever form you choose, come, come!

But the same couplet is attributed to other Sufis, as well. As far as we know, Sarmad's little collection of *ruba'iyyat* (translated by Zahurul Hassan Sharib, [Southampton, 1994]) is his only work.

SHAH DA'I SHIRAZI

Nizamoddin Mahmud Dā'i Shirāzi, "Shāh Dā'i", was born 810/1406–7 and died 870/1464–65 in Shiraz. He was a member of a number of Sufi orders, but his chief initiation was from Shāh Ne'matollāh Wali (q.v.), whom he represented as shaykh of Shiraz. For a full account of his life and works, including translations of a number of poems, see our *Kings of Love*.

SHAH JAHANGIR HASHEMI

Sayyed Mir Mohammad Hāshem was born in 873/1468–69 of an

aristocratic family of Kerman, descended from Qasem Anwār and Shāh Ne'matollāh Wali (q.v.). (See *Kings of Love*.) In his youth he emigrated to Sindh to study Sufism, and his reputation is greater there than in Persia. In 946/1539–40 he was killed by bandits on his way to Mecca. He wrote a *diwān* and a *mathnawi, Mazhar al-āthār*.

SHAH NE'MATOLLAH WALI

Shāh Nuroddin Ne'matollāh Wali was born in Aleppo in 731/1331. After much travel in search of a master, he met the famous Qādiri/Shādhili Sufi and historian, Abdollāh Yāfi'i, in Mecca and was initiated by him. He met the Mongol conqueror Timurlane. He settled in Kerman and died near there in the village of Mahan in 834/1431, having initiated literally hundreds of thousands of disciples. The order named after him is today the largest and most important in Iran. (See *Kings of Love*.)

WAHSHI BAFQI

Wahshi Bāfqi was born near Kerman. He taught primary school in Kashan for some time, then settled in Yazd, where he died in 991/1583. Legend has it he was killed by a girl he loved. A prolific poet, he composed in all genres, including panegyrics to Shah Tamasp.

Peter Lamborn Wilson and Nasrollah Pourjavady's *Kings of Love: The Poetry and History of the Ni'matullāhi Sufi Order of Iran* (Tehran, 1978) includes about a hundred translations of poems by masters and disciples of a single Persian Sufi order. P. L. Wilson has collaborated with G. R. Aavani on *Nasir-i Khusraw: Forty Poems from the Divan* (Tehran, 1977); with B. M. Weischer on *Heart's Witness: The Sufi Quatrains of Awhaduddin Kermāni* (Tehran, 1979); and with. K. Schlamminger on *Weaver of Tales: Persian Picture Carpets* (Munich, 1980). He is also author of *Angels* (London and New York, 1980); *Scandal: Essays in Islamic Heresy* (Autonomedia, 1988); and *Sacred Drift: Essays on the Margins of Islam* (City Lights, 1993).